PLAYER
hateHER

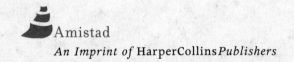

Amistad
An Imprint of HarperCollins*Publishers*

Player hateHER

How to Avoid the Beat Down and Live in a Drama-Free World

TAMARA A. JOHNSON-GEORGE

and KATRINA R. CHAMBERS

HarperCollins books may be purchased for educational, business, or sales promotional use. For information please write: Special Markets Department, HarperCollins Publishers, 10 East 53rd Street, New York, NY 10022.

FIRST EDITION

Designed by Janet M. Evans

Library of Congress Cataloging-in-Publication Data has been applied for.

ISBN 978-0-06-112572-0

08 09 10 11 12   OV/RRD   10 9 8 7 6 5 4 3 2 1

This book is dedicated
to our mothers:

Gwendolyn C. Pegram

and

Cathy G. Chambers

CONTENTS

PLAYER
hateHER

Introduction

Player hater *is a term from the late sixties used to describe* a person criticizing a mack, someone with all the power over the finest women. A "cool cat," if you will. To celebrate the true players, there were fancy players' balls. At these functions the Mack of the Year would be crowned. Those players who lost would secretly be livid, thus, player hating and finding every flaw with the new mack. We have taken the term *player hater* and redirected it toward anyone and everything—especially women. Every day women players hate one another instead of embracing one another. That's how the idea of *Player hateHER* came to be.

TAMARA: Katrina and I lived totally and completely different lives before we crossed each other's path. I guess that's what makes us so compatible. We're not so much opposites as twins raised in two totally different environments.

I am Tamara Antrice Johnson-George, better known to most as Taj of the group SWV. Being in SWV, a popular group back in the day, was the biggest highlight of my life. Growing up, I didn't have much. It seemed like my family struggled through every year. One thing I did have was my mother and my three older brothers. We always made one another laugh; it was our special remedy for whatever we didn't have. I always liked to sing, but I never thought it would take me so far. Through my association with SWV I have met so many different types of people and learned so much from them. I absorbed a little piece of everyone while still seeking my individual goals outside of SWV.

I met Katrina through a mutual friend, and we clicked instantly. She was funny and sincere. I felt like I had found a little piece of my family in her. We would talk on the phone for literally hours about everything from whatever diet we were currently on, to the men in our lives, to the African dance class I was taking, straight through to all of our dreams and aspirations. We just clicked. We filled a void in each other's life.

Katrina grew up in a comfortable, two-parent home with her brother. Very popular and athletic, she was always a group leader among her friends. Her father was in the army, so they traveled a lot. Katrina was an "army brat." She was born in the country and I was born in the city.

Katrina loves the city and I'm ready to settle down in the country. Sometimes I'd fill her in on what life was like when I used to live in New York City, and she was honestly amazed. And then she'd tell me about what life was like for her when she lived in Texas. When she would tell me about holidays in her house, I'd be so touched because it was exactly the way I always wanted to spend the holidays.

KATRINA: I am Katrina Renee Chambers, affectionately known as Trina. I was born in Kannapolis, North Carolina. My father was in the military, so I spent the majority of my life traveling until he retired to San Antonio, Texas. I guess I had what would be called your typical all-American family: mom, dad, boy, girl. I went to college on a volleyball scholarship and received a Bachelor of Arts degree in communications; my brother followed in my father's footsteps and joined the military. I have always been a very outgoing person, involved in a lot of extracurricular activities, and many of my peers considered me a leader. I thought the life I had lived was pretty much the norm for everybody—that is, until I met Tamara in 1995.

"The Introduction" that brought me to Tamara was one that I will never forget. Arnetta is a girlfriend of mine whom I have known since the seventh grade. She is one of my best friends; we literally grew up together. Arnetta and I have shared in each other's life through our early preteens, college graduations, life in the real world, and on to the birth of her daughter, Taahirah, who also happens to be my goddaughter. So it's safe to say we've become lifelong friends. As we continued through our busy lives trying to act like grown-ups, our circle of friends continued to grow. I will never forget the day that Arnetta called me and told me that she met "Taj" from SWV. I was so excited for her! SWV was one of our favorite groups and I could not believe that she not only met her, but they had actually made plans to hang out. I was happy and jealous all at the same time. Yes, I was player-hating a little bit. But what made me feel a little better was what Arnetta told me next: she said that Taj was really cool and she thought that the two of us would hit it off and she couldn't wait for us to meet the next time I came to visit.

Because of our busy schedules, it would be months before Arnetta, Taj, and I finally hooked up. I was honestly becoming a little agitated that Arnetta was talking about her so much (hating again). What I didn't know was that Arnetta was also talking to Taj about me, just as much. Taj and Arnetta had been hanging out for some time because they were both dating guys who played for the same NBA team. So it wasn't unusual for the two of them to be together during one of my habitual phone calls to Arnetta.

Then it finally happened. All three of us were in New York City at the same time. I was working in Brooklyn and Arnetta had decided to fly up to New York for the weekend to visit Taj. So we arranged to meet for dinner at a restaurant near Taj's condo. At this point, Arnetta had only been at Taj's for two days but she had already called me the day before and told me that Christopher Williams, the legendary R&B crooner himself, lived in Taj's building and that he had come over to visit while she was there. At first, I screamed into the phone because I had seriously fallen in love with Christopher Williams ever since I had seen him in *New Jack City*! And she confirmed everything I already thought I knew: he was just as fine in person and he was sooooooo nice. For some reason, I was beginning to think that Taj was going to be one of those stuck-up entertainers who thought she was all that and everybody else wasn't if they weren't "famous" like her. I had been working as a production manager in the music video industry and had come across a lot of artists whose music I loved, but whose personalities turned out to be just plain ol' rude. I even thought about coming up with some excuse as to why I had to cancel, but I have to admit, there was something telling me that I just had to meet this "Taj from SWV" person. And I did. All I can say is Arnetta was absolutely right. We did hit it off! We greeted each other with hugs, not the traditional handshakes or the standard "nice to meet ya." And there was nothing stuck-up about her, she was and has been one of the most genuine and funniest people I've ever met. It was as if I had known her all my life.

Growing up, I used to dream of having a big sister who I could talk to about anything. And even though Taj is only a year older than me, she has become my big sister. Our backgrounds are so different, yet we share so much. She opened up a world for me that I never knew existed. The Introduction happened over ten years ago and we have been inseparable ever since. It's crazy! And every now and then, we stop and laugh about how amazingly accurate Arnetta was in believing that the two of us would hit it off. And the rest, as they say, is history. . .

Together we have laughed, cried, argued, and, yes, we have player-hated. As a matter of fact, it is one of our favorite pastimes.

Whenever I think about how the concept of *Player hateHER* came to be, I instantly laugh out loud. So many times Tamara and I have spent hours talking about ourselves and our female contemporaries. Those who talk about us, and those we talk about. The end result is always the same; laughter. But too often sisters don't see the humor in the situation, and they begin instantly disliking a woman they don't even know. So, in our player hating, we're not only assessing a situation we know little or nothing about; we are also forfeiting any attempt we may have at forming what could be a lasting friendship.

TAMARA: Yes, we both are guilty of being Player hate-HERs. One summer, while on a business trip in the British Virgin Islands, we really noticed our player-hating ways. There was one particular instance when we were sitting by the pool relaxing and doing a little people watching. We came across an African-American woman sitting alone, also relaxing by the pool. We immediately, almost subconsciously, began to assess this woman. We started with her looks—by our standards, average. Then we wondered why she was even on the islands, where she got the nerve to wear that little bikini, and the fact that she didn't have a man, or so we thought. As it turned out, she not only had a man, but she had a nice-looking *Caucasian* man. After the initial shock wore off, we really started to talk about her. How could she be on this island with a man while two beautiful women like ourselves were alone?

Who did she think she was and what did he possibly see in her?

And to make matters worse, as she got up to leave she stopped and introduced herself to us. Now this suddenly beautiful woman gave us her room number and invited us to hang out with her and her husband (they were honeymooning) if we had the time. She also didn't hesitate to mention how much more comfortable she had felt now that she had met some "sisters" from the States. Needless to say, we felt very small. It was at this moment that the concept of *Player hateHER* came to be.

So, after we finished laughing and telling everyone we knew what had happened, we decided to write a book. We realized that all women player-hate. We player-hate on those we don't know, as well as some of our closest friends. And we have also been the victims of player hating. However, our player hating has never cost us a friendship, as a matter of fact; it has even strengthened a few of them (call it constructive criticism).

KATRINA: But finding this strength in player hating seems to be a rarity because women constantly let jealousy, lies, and rumors divide us all.

And if you really think back, you can find that player hating truly has a rich and famous history. Back in the day it was no secret that Bette Davis and Joan Crawford were envious of each other; or that there was some tension between Diana Ross and fellow Supreme Mary Wilson. Today, we still see this type of player hating, for example: Paris Hilton vs. Nicole Richie, Lindsay Lohan vs. Hilary Duff, Naomi Campbell vs. Tyra Banks, Pink vs. Christina

Aguilera; from *The Apprentice,* Omarosa vs. Ereka Vetrini and Star Jones on *The View* vs. almost all of her costars. We simply don't give one another a chance. As long as we are divided, we are no good; but as women united in sisterhood, we can truly be a force to be reckoned with. This is evident in sororities, clubs, and other social organizations that are composed solely of women. The more we come together, the more we accomplish.

As women, we seem to player-hate on those whom we most admire. So, to all the sisters who have ever been the victim of a Player hateHER; take it as a compliment. Our purpose in writing this book was to bring a world of women closer together, women who are otherwise divided by some of the silliest reasons. We also hope reading it will make you laugh as much as we did while writing it. And as you complete each chapter and get the urge to share your own personal stories of player hating or even just to say hello, visit us at www.playerhateher.com.

One

What Is a Player hateHER?

What is player hating? I'm so glad that you asked. It's a syndrome suffered by most women that attacks our egos without warning, causing us to lash out at other women for the smallest of reasons. Oh, but don't worry, there's definitely a cure for this small, but persistent weakness. You'll probably read about yourself in one of the following chapters; as a matter of fact, we know you will. And don't be afraid to admit that you're a Player hateHER; admission is half the battle. Read on, girl!

KATRINA: A Player hateHER, by our definition, is a woman who unnecessarily displays a negative attitude toward another woman for trivial reasons. For the most part, whenever you openly disagree with another woman's choices in life, such as how she wears her hair, how she chooses to dress, what man she chooses to be with, and the list goes on . . . you're being a Player hateHER. Don't be fooled into thinking you're innocent and excluded from this group; everyone has been a Player hateHER at one time or another, and It could be instigated by anything.

TAMARA: For instance, you're having a get-together at your house and you realize you still need a few extra odds and ends from the grocery store. You think to yourself, let me hurry and get there before the store closes. You're at the grocery store wearing a T-shirt, sweatpants, and a baseball cap. You thought it didn't matter how you looked because you were just making a quick run to the store. While you're in the produce aisle, you notice a woman dressed like a million bucks. She's in her nightclub best with her "all my breasts are revealed" leopard-print tank top, skintight black capri pants, six-inch leopard-print mules to match, and a toe ring for every toe (except the big ones). Immediately you think to yourself, "It's only the grocery store, not dinner and a movie." Lo and behold, woman, you are player-hatin'.

KATRINA: Player hating starts early. On the elementary school playground, little Suzie, who has fancy clothes and "good" hair, talks about little Lisa, who is dressed in hand-me-downs and has more "natural" hair. Suzie says to her friends in a voice, loud enough for Lisa to hear, "Her hair is so nappy!" And laughs out loud with her friends. Thus, the Player hateHER is born. I think everyone can admit that there was a little Suzie and a little Lisa in their school.

There's often some kind of rivalry among females. Sometimes it's subtle, and other times it can be loud enough for the whole world to hear. As long as we long to change something about ourselves or want something the next woman possesses, we will always find fault with a woman who's taking charge of her life.

TAMARA: When I was a child, my family didn't have a lot of money. Every day in school was a living hell for me. I didn't fit into any of the "cliques." I was too "down" for the nerds and too poor to fit in with the fancy girls. So I just bounced along between the lines throughout my school days. The kids at school took advantage of every opportunity to point out my misfortunes. Children can be cruel. Unknowingly, they initiated me into the cycle of player hating.

KATRINA: I, on the other hand, grew up with a lifestyle that could probably best be described as the exact opposite of Tamara's. I was very popular, which I used to my advantage, and with very little effort I had others wanting to join me. While I was struggling to break into the entertainment industry, I often worked as a teacher to generate additional income. Usually, it was as a substitute teacher, but having a bachelor's degree also gave me the opportunity to teach full-time. While working as an educator in the public school system on the elementary, intermediate, and high school level, I was able to see firsthand how detrimental picking on someone who is less fortunate can be. But when I was in school, I certainly didn't realize this. My friends and I could make or break a little girl like Tamara with the simplest of acts. I could lift her spirits up with a simple hello or I could crush that very same spirit by pointing and looking down at her "no name" shoes as I glided by in my brand-new Nike tennis shoes.

As the Player hateHER grows older, her actions become more subtle. When you were a kid you could be blatant, but as an adult, you know that's rude, so now you find more clever ways to player-hate; like whispering, sign language, eye rolling, and of course, staring. However, for adult women, joining a "clique" takes on a whole new meaning. Most of us don't even know that we are a part of one.

✦ Tiffany recalls the time when her college roommate, Lacy, stopped speaking to her because earlier that day she had seen her sitting in the café with Alexis, who had been rumored to be a lesbian. And Lacy was a definite homophobe. She even accused her own boyfriend of being on the "down low" several times throughout their two-year relationship. But this time she went too far: she spoke to the RA to request a new roommate. The next day Tiffany was asked to move out even though Lacy was the one complaining about the living arrangement! Tiffany and Lacy have not spoken to each other since that day. ✦

Let's face it, we all belong to certain groups. We may go from one group to the next on any occasion: from poor to rich, from the church to the club. But no one is exempt from membership in cliques, and as women, we are all a part of this divided society that makes up our player-hating world.

Some women may instantly think this book doesn't apply to them, that they have never player-hated on anyone. But anyone who thinks—I mean really *thinks*—will find that at one time or another she talked about that other woman over there!

Now, you don't need to walk around all paranoid, thinking that everyone is player-hating you. You'll know when it's happening; you'll feel the piercing stare going right through you. Be alert! When you get that feeling, don't be obvious in your reaction. Look around the room inconspicuously. (The Player hateHER could be watching you from a corner, using a magazine as a cover-up!) Once you have spotted the culprit, what do you do?

Read on. The following chapters will educate you on the secret society we call Player hateHERs. The situations are all true. However, we changed the names to protect the guilty!

Two

Why We Player-Hate: Jealousy Equals Insecurity

"Look at her big breasts!"
"I know that's a rent-a-car."
"That is not a real Gucci!"
"Her beautiful hazel eyes are contact lenses."

There is a common thread among Player hateHERs. Most often the people who player-hate on others are intimidated, insecure, and/or jealous about a certain characteristic they see in the person or people they are hating on.

This characteristic is something that they feel they could never possess or gain. Feeling this way makes the hateHER feel inadequate. It is easier for these people to criticize others than to change themselves.

JEALOUSY • Type A
The Visual Hater!

TAMARA: It all starts with the eyes. Before we speak to a woman or are introduced to a woman, we visually size her up, assessing what we like and dislike about her. Subconsciously, whether you know it or not, you are comparing her to yourself. "Her hair is so thick, and mine is too thin to even hold a curl without a perm. If my hair were just a little bit thicker, I'd be the bomb. But not that thick; her hair is probably unmanageable." In reality, if your hair was as thick as hers, you would be able to try many different hairstyles without worry, but thin hair limits you. That's when the what-ifs and only-ifs come in to play.

> "I never like to go into a room full of women alone. If I can help it, I'm always with someone because I feel more comfortable with a crowd. I hate when people stare at me like my shirt is open when I walk into a room."
>
> KATE, *California*

Many women experience this same uncomfortable feeling when they walk into a room full of people, especially a room full of women they are not familiar with. Kate can take comfort in knowing that she is not alone. Here's a tip: whenever I walk into a room, especially if it is crowded, I stare at the wall in front of me while occasionally moving my head from side to side. Moving your head provides the illusion that you are looking at someone in particular and not just nervous out of your mind. This way, your attention is centered and you are able to focus on what you have to do and where you are going.

I always find myself wishing upon a star to have thicker hair, a smaller waist, and smaller hips. I just can't help myself. It seems like every time I run into someone with beautiful thick hair, that little tiny figure or beautiful smooth skin I player-hate. I can admit it. I'm not rude about it . . . just jealous.

If I think a woman has qualities that are better than mine, sometimes I all too quickly tell myself, "It just can't be natural." On the other hand, if she doesn't measure up to my qualifications, I won't see her as a threat to me at all. Sometimes, she's the one I am more likely to befriend simply because I feel a little insecure.

My jealousy can get the best of me; every now and then I can't help but player-hate. How many times have I had a feeling so strong that it caused me to turn around or look over my shoulder? How many times have I asked a girlfriend to accompany me into a room because of the stares I anticipate? It's an uncomfortable feeling, being scrutinized like this. I wonder if my shirt is unbuttoned or my mascara is running. When this uncomfortable emotion arises, I feel the need to protect myself. This is when my player-hating protection mechanism kicks in. I'm no longer the Player hateHER victim; I'm a Player hateHER, too! I begin to pinpoint the things *I* dislike and build a hate-HER shield around myself for protection. Now, I'm in a stand-off with someone I don't even know. And the only thing I can say by way of explanation is "She was looking at me funny."

She may be looking at me suspiciously for any number of reasons; for example, she might really like my hair and want to try my hairstyle. But her stares are misinterpreted as *her* player-hating. In my mind, she's jealous and I feel threatened.

> "I never thought I was a Player hateHER until I went to your Web site. In my mind, I was being helpful when I would tell a girl about herself. When I think about it I might be offended if someone told me about everything that was wrong with me, too."
>
> TANIKA, *Colorado*

On occasion, it is perhaps a good idea to keep our opinions to ourselves. It is my experience that everything about someone doesn't have to be addressed. Often women want to be helpful by telling another that she is not as on point as she might believe herself to be; but it can be misunderstood. Proceed with caution if you must!

JEALOUSY • Type B
Familial Hateration

KATRINA: I know, personally, I get player-hated on all the time when I'm out with my brother, Jay. First, let me explain a little bit about Jay to help you better understand the Player hateHER's point of view. A few years back, before he got married to my beautiful sister-in-law and had my two handsome nephews, he was an educated black man in his late twenties, a soldier in the United States Army, attractive (runs in the family), no babies, and single. But what makes him most attractive to the ladies is that he isn't currently, and never has been incarcerated, doesn't sell drugs, and . . . he isn't attached to any baby's mama. Yes, ladies, he was twenty-eight years old with no kids! Believe me; I do understand that we, as black women, are experiencing what seems to be a shortage of eligible black men. But before you go player-hating on the sister with that nice-looking brother, find out if she really is, in fact, his sister!

And I don't know what was worse, my brother complaining that he wasn't getting any "play" because all the women assumed I was his woman, or the women hating on me because they thought that he was my man. They were jealous and staring at me funny, and for no reason.

Once, I was in a mall with Jay and this woman was staring me down with the most evil look I'd ever seen. I looked all around to see who she was directing this hatred toward, because I had done nothing to warrant an evil eye. But her eyes never left mine. "Oh, snap!" Ol' girl was indeed giving me the evil eye. And when Jay looked her way she displayed a silly, flirtatious smile. Without a clue of the battle that she and I were engaged in, Jay just returned the flirtatious smile. That smile from my brother just confirmed for her what she already knew; that Jay belonged with her and not with me.

I'm not quite sure at what point her snickering and staring at me caused Jay to start looking at her like she was crazy, but she didn't even notice. As far as she was concerned, this fight was between her and me, and the victorious one would take Jay home. This girl was serious (or desperate). I was on the receiving end of some of the worst neck and eye rolling possible. She was rolling her eyes so far up into her head, I thought for sure they were going to get stuck. Then it happened. This heifer mumbled some rude obscenity and then sucked her teeth at me. I couldn't take it anymore, the game was over: "He's my brother!" I shouted. It truly amazes me how suddenly a Player hateHER can turn that same rolling neck into a lovely platform for her now warm and inviting "how you doin', girlfriend, let's make friends" smile. But by this time, it was too late, because I had already begun to show my attitude.

Meanwhile she had walked over to us and tried to explain to me that it was "that time of the month" and, at the same time, tried to slip Jay her phone number. We were both too busy to pay her any attention. Jay was busy pulling me away while I was busy telling her (in a most calm and dignified way, of course) that she had just played herself.

> "When I was younger my older brother used to take me to the clubs with him. We are only two years apart, so many of the women in the club would think we were there together as a couple instead of my big brother keeping an eye on me.

It used to drive me crazy how those girls would stare me down and be so nasty until they found out I was his sister. I knew it wasn't right, but I would have an attitude at that point. It serves them right for being so unnecessarily rude."

CRYSTAL, *Indiana*

I suggest that you fight fire with fire only as your last resort. Crystal says she was never given an opportunity to tell those rude women she encountered that her "companion" was indeed her brother. Now that we've covered two types of jealousy, we can see there are many forms of it. Our instincts to endow a woman with qualities she doesn't possess; judging a woman as a lover when she is merely a sister or best friend—these are situations that can work against us in serious ways. There are also times when our jealousy can actually hurt someone's feelings and work to undermine someone's confidence. This brings us to Jealousy Type C.

JEALOUSY • Type C
Club Hating

KATRINA: When you step into a club looking great, you know it. Earlier in the week you were at the gym looking in the mirror at yourself, admiring the shape you're in, and now you're at the club and the fellas are noticing, too. You are feeling good because all those evenings spent in the gym are finally reaping some serious rewards. One by one they ask for a dance and you graciously offer a proud "yes" and your hand with each request. After all, you did not spend five hours at the beauty salon to hold up the wall (your appointment was at 10 a.m., but you didn't hit the chair till noon). When you finally do decide to sit down and take a break from dancing, they're the first ones you notice: the Player hateHERs. Unbeknownst to you, they have been checking you out all night long. From the moment you stepped into the doorway, the men were staring with approval. They noticed you giving cute little hugs and kisses to those you knew, and they noticed the exchange of cute little smiles with those you didn't know.

It wasn't too long before you entered the club that the Player hateHERs had walked through the same door; however, they did not receive the same reaction. Some guys looked up, but then it turned out that they were actually looking up and *over* them. And those women had been there long enough for somebody/anybody to have sent over a drink or asked for a dance. Since that didn't happen, it's entirely your fault. But, ladies, it's confidence. Confidence is the key. If you exude a certain amount of confidence in yourself and in everything that you do, it will attract others.

> "I met my best friend at a club. She and I were the only two people willing to get on the dance floor while everyone else was holding up the wall. We laughed and talked and danced for hours. We still make it a habit to do this eight years later."
>
> SARA, *Ohio*

Tamara and I are the same way. We will dance and have fun anywhere we go because we are confident in ourselves. I am my own biggest fan. I believe I can do anything I set my mind to. And if you doubt me, you have only challenged me; and I hate to lose. You cannot tell me that I, Katrina Renee Chambers, am not cute. Just refer to the picture on the back of this book (I can just see all the Player hateHERs turning up their faces right about now). And you're probably cute, too, but I may not get around to telling you, so you have to tell yourself.

Tamara's the same way. We'll go to the mall and she'll try on an outfit, step out of the dressing room, and say, "I'm cute, right?" I'll say "no", she'll say "thanks," and then purchase her outfit. Next, it's my turn. I step out of the dressing room and say, "Does this make me look fat?" She'll say "yes", I'll say "thanks," and proceed to make my purchase. Then we move on to the next store and repeat the ritual. When we finally do leave the mall we both have bags of fabulous outfits that look great on us. As friends, we wouldn't let each other go out looking crazy, but as Player hateHERs, we won't admit it.

Now, let me get back to what I was saying about the Player hateHERs at the club. You're continuing to dance with almost every guy who asks and you are really enjoying yourself on this well-deserved night out. Then it happens: while you are sipping on the drink that your last dance partner sent over to your table, you realize you have to go to the bathroom. Even though your night has been going great, you dread this moment. You have to pass by this table full of women who have been staring "in your grill" all night. Determined not to let these ladies ruin your night, you decide to just ignore them.

Hah! Easier said than done. As you approach their table their heads are all joined together like a group of Siamese twins and they're laughing, ridiculously loud. As you move closer to their table, the outright laughing becomes quiet snickering, accompanied by the obvious finger-pointing. And as you pass by, the whispering becomes more of a dull roar, all of which, of course, you can hear. And there's always that one Player hateHER who blurts out, "She ain't all that!"

If you ignore the Player hateHER, you only upset her, so you can expect company in the ladies' room. However, the Player hateHER has all the courage of a flea. So she will rarely, if ever, say anything directly to you. Instead, inside the ladies' room, you will be treated to more of the same neck rolling and snickering. The best thing to do is just do what you gotta do—tighten up your hair and makeup, then go back out there and get your groove on!

At the end of the night, when the deejay calls for the last dance, the sister who came to the club to get her groove on will be exchanging phone numbers with her dance partner. The Player hateHERs will be looking puzzled, trying to figure out where all the time went. It takes a lot more time and energy to player-hate than it does to just have a good time. Player hateHERs let jealousy and pettiness ruin what was supposed to be a fun night out on the town.

The victim of all the player hating could have used that pettiness to boost her confidence by realizing that player hating is an immature form of admiration. However, the sad reality is that she probably went home with a lot of insecurities. As hard as she might have tried to just simply enjoy herself, in all honesty it is hard to ignore criticism from our peers! With every dance step this woman was wondering if her hair was okay, if her skirt made her butt look too big, and what on earth could be causing these women to laugh at her. All because a group of ladies decided to Player hateHER!

Take it from a newly reformed Player hateHER like myself: I used to go out quite a bit, but after a while I wasn't enjoying the clubs as much. I realized that I was sabotaging my own fun by sitting at a table player-hating when I should have been out on the dance floor gettin' my groove on.

Player hating is reciprocal. You've most likely been both a victim and perpetrator. None of us are exempt, but if there is one thing that is consistent, it's that usually the people we player-hate have some quality or characteristic that we want to have even if we choose not to admit it. Most Player hateHERs are just insecure with themselves or intimidated by what they don't understand. They don't realize that they already possess that certain quality, or can easily obtain it. It's easier to criticize others than to change ourselves.

Three

Men: The Reoccurring Root of Player Hating

"That's his girlfriend?!"
"She's not all that."

If we are honest with ourselves, we can admit that the most vindictive form of player hating almost always involves a man. There are some men who might be worth a fight, but there has to be a better way. For generations, women have rolled their eyes, sucked their teeth, and bickered senselessly over men. Women tend to align themselves either on the side of the woman who has been cheated on, or on that of the woman who is perceived to be taking the latter's man. In fact both women are actually the victims, and the culprit is the cheating man.

> "After my girlfriend and her husband divorced, his new wife thought she could just jump into the everyday program that my girlfriend used to do. She tried hanging out with all of my girlfriend's friends and having her kids in the same programs. I made it very clear who had my loyalty. I treated her like the home wrecker she is."
>
> ROBIN, *Texas*

TAMARA: Like Robin, many of us decide to choose sides when a couple we know splits up. The best way for Robin to help her recently divorced friend is to be a strong support system. Many women deal with issues of insecurity and low self-esteem when dealing with a cheating husband or boyfriend and allow irrational thoughts to cloud their minds. Robin can help her friend maintain a level head by staying as neutral as possible in spite of her feelings of animosity toward the new wife. The last thing she should do is add fuel to the fire by overtly taking sides. Let's stop player-hating *one another* and direct more scrutiny toward *the men*. Who is really to blame? I think we know the answer to that question.

When a man cheats on his significant other, almost instinctively she will want to attack the girl. "How could he be with her? She's ugly, she's fat and stupid." Any putdown will seemingly relieve your pain, but probably everything he likes about her is something you think you probably lack. That makes you feel insecure and angry. Rather than confronting him about how the attention he gives to other women makes you feel, it is easier for you to direct your anger toward the woman.

> "When I heard my boyfriend's voice mail with an-
> other woman's voice telling him everything that
> I say to him ("I love you," "I miss you," "see you
> at the house"), all I wanted to do was find her
> and kick her @#$%. But when I sat down and
> thought about it, I really couldn't think of one
> thing that she had actually done to me. It was
> his cheating @#$%!"
>
> TARA, *Tennessee*

Tara was infuriated, but eventually she took a more level-headed approach to her situation. Her first instinct was to call the woman; instead she collected all of her boyfriend's personal belongings that he had left at her house and threw them in her trash compactor. When he finally came to her house, she broke up with him and never looked back.

Men will do whatever they are allowed to do. We collected over thirty responses from our Web site and focus groups to the question "Would you stay with a man who has cheated on you?" Surprisingly, twenty-three of the women said that they would stay if their husband/boyfriend cheated. When asked why, most of them replied with the same response. They were either tired of starting over, felt that they wouldn't be able to get another man, or just didn't have the confidence to sever the relationship.

This takes us back to the insecurity and low-self-esteem issues that women suffer from. How many women do you think would fare better against a cheating partner if they thought the world of themselves? All too often, a strong, confident woman is labeled "stuck-up," "conceited," or "full of herself" when she stands up for herself.

It is sometimes hard being different from the pack. The women in our poll were very brave to admit that they would stay in a less-than-stellar relationship. It is equally important to know that only you will know your strengths. If it takes you a lifetime to figure them out and build up enough heart to end your dead-end relationship, then so be it. When you are strong enough to stand on your own, you'll be a role model for other women struggling with the same issue.

> **"I lived with a guy for about six months. The relationship ended because he said I was too bossy and demanding. How is telling him what I want and how I like things too bossy? Should I have just said nothing? One of us had to go and all I know is that I still have the same apartment."**
>
> PETRANELLA, *New York*

Petranella made a firm move, but no one can expect everything to go their way all the time. Maybe try setting some beginner boundaries such as housecleaning duties and go from there. It is unfair to expect someone, unless you gave birth to them, to live completely by your rules all the time, especially a grown man.

A big problem for women is the belief that there are only a few good men out there to choose from. There are plenty of men out there to go around (I'm sure of it!). Think about a car; if a car breaks down, you try to get it fixed, but after a while you can't keep investing your money in a lost cause. And relationships can be treated the same way. In the end, you'll save money on your car as well as money from sympathy shopping.

> "I took a guy back after he cheated on me twice. It seemed like the more I would forgive him the more he would cheat on me. It got so bad that he was cheating on me in our home. That's when I realized that this guy could care less about me. I finally broke up with him for good after he looked me in my eyes and swore that he would never cheat again and not even a week later I found him kissing some girl in his car. I said enough is enough!"
>
> STACY, *Illinois*

Once you have given your best and your best is not good enough to hold the relationship together, it's time to let go. Even if you love your partner with all your heart, if they're not treating you with love and respect, let them go. Things can only get better once you've dropped that deadweight.

If you have ever been in this situation, I'm sure that you can relate to the emotional head trip a cheating guy can put you through. Unfortunately, I speak from years of experience. After kissing several frogs, hoping for a prince, I learned to separate the frogs from the princes. Now I have a sixth sense and the ability to spot a mistake in advance. I've learned to recognize the flirtatious committed guys by their ambiguity. I can spot the multi-girlfriend guys by their willingness to do anything. Occasionally I can pinpoint a decent guy with potential by his manners alone. Take the time to figure out what you are working with so that you can avoid being put in a situation where you might end up getting hurt and then projecting your anger onto the wrong person.

Women need to realize that when a man cheats, the *man* is the guilty party, not the other woman! These men are playing both of you for their own selfish needs because it is convenient. Don't listen to his sorry excuses, like, "It just happened."

> **"My boyfriend put his hand on a stack of Bibles and told me that he never meant for anything to happen; he just wanted a friend."**
>
> PAIGE, *Tennessee*

I have six older brothers, and excluding the three who are happily married, I have been schooled in the ways of men by three of the sweetest, but doggish men around. They always told me: every time an unfamiliar man approaches you in a way that is not platonic, already before he says hello, he's undressed you. You know who the wrongdoer is in a situation like this. So, why are we attacking one another? Regrettably, every now and then a guy may come off as an innocent bystander. There are some trifling women out there who *will* gladly cut your throat, so to speak, to get your man.

> "My so-called best friend couldn't wait for me to turn my back long enough for her to approach my boyfriend. I don't trust anyone around my boyfriends now, not even my sisters."
>
> TOI, *Maryland*

Let's get real: you shouldn't care if another woman seals herself to your man with Krazy Glue. *He knows* he already has a woman; his response should be "No thanks, I'm involved," or plain and simply "Hell, no!" Seriously, some men think that they are so slick.

> "After I caught my boyfriend cheating on me, I called the girl and had a very pleasant talk with her. I told her that I wasn't mad at her at all and I told her all about his bad habits. I also told her that if he cheated on me with her, he would do the same thing to her with someone else. We are actually still cordial to each other."
>
> LAURA, *Georgia*

This is a great example of how to change a negative situation into a positive one. If this happens to you, take a moment to clear your head and breathe before you react. Your reaction will be totally different than if you were to blow your top.

Long before I met my husband, Eddie, Katrina and I were working on this book and laughing it up when the cutest guy walked in and sat directly across from our table at our favorite Barnes & Nobles in Jersey City. I'd say he was about six two, lean and rugged. He was wearing baggy fleece shorts with an oversize T-shirt with the sleeves cut off. Ladies, he was definitely a looker.

Being the woman that I am, I looked in his direction to get his attention. I know, I know. That was real corny, but it worked. Once I got his attention, I asked him with my sweetest Halle Berry voice, "What are you reading?" I could sense he was flattered by my approach. He gave me a sexy chuckle and replied, "The newspaper." I'm thinking oh, yeah. Quickly, I come back with "Read the horoscopes. I'm a Taurus and I match with every sign. You can call me Taj and I'm very happy to meet you." Yes, I'm extremely corny, but again, it got his attention. I stretched my arm out with my hand in the kissing position for him to kiss it or at least shake it, when I almost swallowed my tongue. Mr. Rugged was wearing a wedding band.

> "I always check hands, wrists, necks, and wallets for any sign of marriage or family before I get too happy with a man. You just never know. Even if they don't have on a physical ring, check their ring finger for ring marks. Some men will lie."
>
> CHASTITY, *Texas*

I snatched my hand back so fast that I beat the speed of light by two seconds. I said in a very firm voice, "So, you're married." Trina exploded with laughter. I can't stand her sometimes. I'm positive she saw his wedding band the minute he walked in. I wear glasses! I'm sure of it because we are like two peas in a pod when it comes to fine men. I thought it was strange she'd just let me have him to myself.

I'll admit to a lot of things, but a mistress, I am not! My attention dried up so fast I forgot he was even sitting there. We finished our writing session for the day and went on about our usual business. I usually parked my car in front of the bookstore to keep a close eye on it. From outside the store, everyone could see you inside, and vice versa. As I got into my car, I took one last damn peek at the handsome specimen of a man and then drove off.

The next day I had to run a few errands. I didn't get home until after 6 P.M. The concierge in my building informed me that someone had left a note for me. Not to brag, but my building is a very nice place to live: spacious condominiums, twenty-four-hour doorman, pools, sauna, gym facility, recreation room, and tennis courts. I've never been more proud of where I lived. I didn't get a chance to read the note right away because my hands were filled with packages. I finally settled down and read the note: *Please call Sgt. Brooks at the Chelsea Police Dept.* The first thing that came to my mind was what the hell did I do?

> **"All of the police officers that I've met have always been married. Most of them are for the tax break. Avoid cute cops at all cost."**
>
> GWEN, *New York*
> (She just may be onto something.)

Then I started to think about the time I switched lanes in the Lincoln Tunnel and wondered if I had run a red light the previous week. I've always seen those signs that say SPEED CHECKED BY RADAR or LANE JUMPERS WILL BE TICKETED, but I never paid them much attention because I had never been busted.

I decided I wouldn't go easy. I didn't call Sergeant Brooks back. If he wanted me he'd have to come and get me. Then I crumpled the paper up into a ball and did a Michael Jordan jump shot and banked it into the trash. The next day the administration department of the building association called me to tell me that a Sergeant Brooks called for me twice that afternoon. My bladder became so weak that I'm positive that I dropped a pinch of urine in my pants. They really were coming to get me! I didn't want the building association to know I was in trouble. I took the message and said, "I already gave to the policeman's ball" as I scurried to the bathroom. Just knowing I was really in trouble seemed to put pressure on my bladder. I couldn't hide anymore; I had to return the call.

I'd decided to play the innocent role and tell him I just got his message today and called back as soon as I could. Now I was lying to the law. When would I learn! As I dialed each number my hand trembled harder and harder. Crazy thoughts were going through my head. I started thinking about a jail for women that would be like HBO's *Oz*. I would never survive. Before I could complete my last thought, I took a deep breath, calmly stated my name, and asked for Sergeant Brooks. "Hello, Miss Johnson." I was about to confess to running that red light when he began to talk. To my surprise, he asked me if I remembered the guy I had met at the bookstore. Now I was lost. Either that guy was a criminal or he had pressed charges against me for just plain harassment even though we barely touched. It definitely was not sexual! I was about to lie and say no, but something told me not to make matters worse, tell the truth. I said yes. I almost did a cartwheel with the phone in my hand when he identified himself as the guy from Barnes & Noble.

After I secretly congratulated myself for snagging such a cutie, I remembered two things: 1) the guy was married, and 2) I never gave him my phone number. Then it hit me, my license plate. That's why he couldn't call me directly. I had just changed my number and my registration still had the old number. I had to give him an A for effort because he didn't give up at a disconnected number. He went as far as to call my building association to find me.

> "I was overwhelmed by how much effort a guy put in to get my attention. I was equally over-whelmed when his wife began calling my house at all times of the night cursing at me for mess-ing with her husband."
>
> KRISTIN, *Ohio*

Kristin was given false information by a married man. After I realized that the handsome man from the book-store was married, I could relate to this story personally. Initially, I, too, enjoyed the flattery from my cop friend.

"Wow, you checked my plates to find me? I don't know

whether to be flattered or afraid." He said, "I'll never admit to that, but you should be both." That to me sounded like a serial killer's comment. I stored it in my mental notebook. Sergeant Brooks and I talked for a few minutes then we set up a lunch date for the next day, which I had every intention of canceling.

About three weeks later, as Trina and I were pulling up to the bookstore, our usual parking space by the front window was occupied by a maroon Acura. After we cursed the guy who stole *our* space, we moved on to find a spot a couple of spaces away. We went inside, took our usual seats, and began our routine of talking about all the folks who passed by us. Trina stood up to stretch her legs when she noticed a gorgeous guy helping his pregnant wife and young son into the same maroon Acura that stole our parking space. She said, "Oh, how cute." I was shocked when I noticed it was Sergeant Brooks, and his family. For some reason, we caught each other's eye and exchanged a pleasant but inconspicuous smile when I stood up to peek out the window. Just like a woman, with her hormones doing backflips, his wife looked at him and then at me. And as she was tracing our exchange of pleasantries, she rolled her eyes so hard at me, I rubbed my forehead to see if there was a hole in it. It was clearly a warning: "He's mine, bitch!" I just chuckled and turned away. That woman had no idea to what lengths her husband had gone to get my attention, but she instantly assumed I was after her man. Yes, I was at first, but I dropped the chase when I found out he was married. Meanwhile, he was acting like the stalker cop from hell. For a brief moment I wanted to create a scene to teach him a lesson, but I didn't want to cause his wife any undue stress in her delicate condition; plus, I would never stoop that low.

· · ✦ · ·

I wish that this was my only unpleasant experience with a guy, but I remember a situation a few years ago with my ex-boyfriend that was equally bad. We were together for three and a half years. For the most part, I thought he was a good man. He was tall, handsome, and a lot of fun. I thought I was special to him until I found out he was considered a five-star pimp all over the East Coast. I was trying to make it work, but he was a D-O-G.

One night his sister called me because she felt I would be able to talk some sense into him. She informed me that he was having a "secret" pool party and had invited about seventy-five of his female acquaintances. I would always tell him how unfair it would be to me if he were seen screwing around, because at that time SWV still had a very high profile in the media. His female friends would always know me, but I wouldn't know them from a hole in the wall. They could come up to me and slap me cross-eyed, or be really cool to me just because they knew who I was and I didn't know who they were. But did he listen? No! As I said before, you can only fix a broken car so many times before you have to just get rid of it.

I was at the nail salon when I received this call from his sister. She sounded really upset; it was obvious she had been crying. Naturally concerned, I knew I had to go check up on him. It was about a four-hour drive from my house in New Jersey to where he was in Washington, D.C., and I was still at the nail salon trying to get a fill. I didn't even let the nice nail technician finish my nails. I just handed her my money and ran to the garage where my car was parked, with no color and only four nails filled. I made it to D.C. around 10:30 P.M. and drove straight to the hotel where he was having his party.

The minute I walked into the lobby, I knew who the guests were. The stares I received were like X-ray vision. The lobby was full of scantily dressed women. I could tell they were criticizing my wardrobe, which was a white tank top and blue Adidas, and sweatpants with white stripes. My hair was in boxed braids, pulled back into a ponytail. I had no makeup on. For God's sake, I had just been going to get my nails done! I overheard one of the girls say, "SWV must not be making any money." For them, laughing out loud became a pastime. In just one short walk through the lobby, those women looked at me and decided they hated my guts. They were player-hating the very blood in my veins because they knew that there was a slight possibility that my then-boyfriend would attempt to snap out of his purple haze and attend to me for even a moment.

I went to use the pay phone in the hotel and experienced the brunt of player hating at its best. The girl who seemed to be the leader of the pack decided to use the phone as well. She knew exactly who I was there to see, but she never acknowledged me. She grabbed the receiver right next to mine so she could listen to my conversation.

She dialed her number and began conversing immediately. Strange, since normally you need to let the phone ring before you start talking (Acting 101).

She was talking into the receiver as if she were "Ms. IT," in total control. "Okay, hurry up. I'm not going to wait here all night, okay, bye." Then she hung up the phone and gave me a smirk, like she had just defeated me. I just laughed at her weak attempt at spying. Then I took pride in myself. I was the focus of these women's attention for that moment, which meant that I was not as bad off as I thought. Somebody cared about my presence. Even if it was a few heifers!

Once my about-to-be ex arrived at the hotel, all of the women practically fell over themselves in order to greet the Man of the Hour, or should I say the Mack-Pimp of the Year? It looked as if they were racing to give him the news of my arrival, as if the one who told him first would get a gold star. He and I started arguing about all that I had been forced to witness that night. I told him I couldn't believe how immature he was behaving. He told me that I held him back because he loved to be around beautiful black women and I wouldn't let him do that. Whenever I would ask about his secret party and all of the women, he would be extremely evasive or just ignore my questions altogether. I was so upset I began to shout out my rage. "Why the hell would you do something like this knowing it would embarrass me? How could you say you love me? What have I done to deserve this?" He never really answered any of my questions. It was almost as if I had been talking to myself. Disappointment was just a small fraction of the bruised emotions I was feeling. It was becoming more and more difficult to focus on his antics with his stable of women watching and laughing out loud at my disenchantment in him. I guess they felt like they were winning something special.

As I began to walk away, I heard someone call my name. When I turned around, one of his friends asked me with a smile on his face, "Mommy, are you mad?" I held my head up high and showed no emotion as I cringed with hurt inside and simply replied, "Yes." One by one, they all tried something different to get under my skin. One girl hung on his every word. She practically wrapped herself around his neck like a necklace. Another girl directed everything she had to say to him even if she was talking to someone else. Then there was another girl who cupped his face in her hands, as if she were holding a delicate flower. They all called his name out, like cats in heat, every other minute. And that creep enjoyed every second of this. While he and I were talking, there were about a dozen "emergencies." Finally, the women became irritated because they couldn't control his attention. They sent one of his friends over to demand that he leave with them. They were all ready to caravan to the club.

Needless to say, for me it was a very long and uncomfortable night. Our relationship ended that night, and I gladly let them all have their party in peace. Although I was very hurt, I walked away with at least some of my self-respect. Believe it or not, I wasn't even mad at those women. As a matter of fact, I felt bad for them. Obviously, no one had told them what they were worth. They deserved to be more than just a number in one man's selfish world.

• • ◆ • •

Our instincts are usually right when it comes to our men and cheating, but on occasion we get it wrong and our player hating isn't only silly, but potentially harmful to our own relationships.

> "When my boyfriend and I started dating, he was so close to one of his female friends from intermediate school it was uncomfortable for me. They are like Julia Roberts and the guy from the movie *My Best Friend's Wedding*. I didn't trust her at first, but after we spent some time together, I realized that she was harmless and she just wanted the best for him."
>
> NICOLE, *Ohio*

It is very possible for a man and a woman to have a platonic relationship. Use your better judgment to assess the situation before you accuse someone of tampering with your goods.

KATRINA: There are about two or three women I have very close friendships with. However, I cannot list my friends without including my homeboys. I have a great relationship, purely platonic, with a male friend, who I'll call Keith. He is like a brother to me. Still, his girlfriend—I'll call her Regina—refuses to believe that we are not having sex. She is so jealous of me, and she has absolutely no reason to be. If only she knew (or should I say believed, because we've already told her a million times) that we spend the majority of our time talking about her! He is crazy in love with her. But she is so jealous of our friendship that she doesn't even realize that she's pushing away a terrific man.

As a matter of fact, before she and Keith got serious, he and I sat down and had a long talk about her. He told me that he was really enjoying her company, how beautiful he thought she was, and the man was smiling from ear to ear. "Damn! You are really cheesin', you are sweating her," I said. It was obvious he was falling for her and I told him to follow his heart and he did. All was well until I met the little (ooops, I almost started hating) . . . until I met Regina. My Player hateHER alarm should've gone off the moment she said, "So, you're *Trina*. Keith talks about you all the time." "That's my bbooyyeee!" I replied as I playfully gave Keith a shove. "Do you have a boyfriend, Trina?" Uh-oh, her fake smile was fading fast now. Keith failed to mention to her that his FRIEND was single. That did it. I was, in no time, no longer just a close friend of Keith's; I was now the reason why they weren't married with two children, a house in the suburbs, and living happily ever after.

Keith and I were friends long before the two of them even met. We are now and will forever be a part of each other's life. I have been with Keith through numerous girlfriends and one baby's mama, and he has seen me through just as many boyfriends. None of these facts seemed to stop her from being a Player hateHER. She doesn't like a single thing about me, yet when the three of us are together, she tries to act like my very best friend. I can't stand that. I know for a fact that she doesn't like me, yet she wants Keith to believe that she and I are the best of friends. However, when we are out without Keith, it's a totally different story, especially when she's with some of her friends; it's like I don't even exist. It's a crazy cycle.

Keith has confided in me on several occasions that he loves her dearly, but that her pettiness and jealousy are driving him away. What she needs to understand is that if Keith cares about *me* so much and she cares about *him* so much, then I must be a good person. Her jealousy isn't allowing her to get to know me the way Keith knows me. She could even find out that the two of us actually have a lot in common. But she is missing the most obvious thing that we have in common, that we both care about—Keith.

> "I can admit when I am wrong. I falsely accused my ex-boyfriend's female best friend of trying to steal my man. I truly regret my accusations because it turned out that she was going through some serious issues and he was only trying to help her. My actions strained our relationship to the point that we broke up and I really regret losing him."
>
> WILENE, *Nevada*

Keith and I will always be close. We are childhood friends; a bond like that is not easily broken. I respect the fact that Regina is Keith's girlfriend, and if she would respect our friendship in the same way instead of player-hating, we would all have a better relationship. Bottom line, Keith will always be my ace, and through association she's my ace's girlfriend! We must learn to get along.

Four

So You Think the Woman Has Everything!

"She thinks she's all that."
"I wouldn't try that if I were her."
"She's showing too much body."

How often have you heard someone say something like that? If you listen carefully, you've probably heard it often. It is usually heard when two or more women are together having lunch or just simply enjoying each other's company. It is usually thought of as a "conversation warmer." This chapter will explore how and why most women think the other woman has everything!

TAMARA: I hear all the time about women who have their act together. It is so refreshing to see women making strides in business as well as their personal lives. I was so overwhelmed after the 2006 midterm elections when California congresswoman Nancy Pelosi became the first female Speaker of the House. That's basically two steps away from the presidency. How incredible for women all across the world.

There are so many positive things happening for women. There is also a side that is not so positive. For instance, as a little girl, I can remember saying things like "Let's not be her friend" or "Don't speak to her because I don't like her." In my teens, my behavior became more extreme. I was usually a loner but eventually became part of a clique. My behavior reflected that of my clique. Needless to say, I wasn't always the nicest person all the time.

> "When I was in college I was always with the 'in' crowd. I felt like I had to do and be like the other girls I hung out with even if we were picking on people. I sometimes felt bad but I tried not to be so mean or rude to people personally. I just tried to fit in."
>
> DANYALE, *Maryland*

It is sometimes easier to fit in than to be an outcast. Danyale is not alone. I, too, felt that way. Within my clique, we would target girls we thought were weaker than us or those we thought we were better than. As I grew older I realized what I was doing. And perhaps, after having my behavior turned on me, I knew that I shouldn't behave like that any longer. I slowly began to separate myself from the cliques and focused more on becoming the person I am today.

> "I used to work out all the time before I had my son. I would always wear a sports bra and a pair of shorts during the warm months and sweats during the cold months. They made me comfortable and I could be as messy as I wanted to be. One day I showed up at my girlfriend's house wearing a sundress, and before she said hello she said to me, "This is the most I've ever seen you wear, what's the occasion?" It bothered me so much that I didn't stay long. I felt like she always had a problem with the way I dressed and never said anything; sort of like she thought less of me. I kind of avoided her for a while. Her tone to me was very condescending and I didn't think it was necessary."
>
> NARISSA, *California*

Narissa should take her girlfriend's comments in stride. Most people say things that will make them feel better. When Narissa's friend saw her in that sundress, her thoughts were probably more along the lines of "I wish I could wear all of the things she can." Narissa's friend saw her own flaws instead of her potential.

Most women can give you a list of everything they believe to be their physical flaws. The flaws that they see are usually transparent to the person looking at them. These perceived flaws give life to our insecurities. Let me be honest; if I didn't see every flaw I think I have, there would be no reason to write this book because in my eyes I'd be perfect and I really wouldn't care how anyone felt about me. But in reality, when I look in the mirror or try on new clothes (especially since I've had my son), I notice every flaw. I always complain about my weight (too much), my hair (too thin), my face (too flat), and I have too much cellulite, and the list goes on and on. Every time I look in the mirror, I see a walking bag of errors that God gave me to figure out. So I do my best to disguise these "flaws" with a little makeup and a hot outfit or whatever will help boost my confidence. So when I step outside I receive compliments first, then maybe a little player hating on the side.

Everyone has flaws. There was only one perfect person born and none of us are it. It is okay to admire someone else's style and what they may have, but when we become envious, therein lies the problem.

> "One thing that I can admit is that I'm a jealous person. It's not that I want everything or I hate everybody. I know that I'm the problem. Whenever I see a girl and she has on something nice or she's got it together, I always wonder how I would look with that or I find the reason why she can do a particular cut or outfit and I can't. I'm working on myself, but I have a long way to go before I stop hating. At least I can admit it, though. Admittance is half the battle and I'm on my way."
>
> JUANITA, *Washington*

Women can't help but notice when another woman has it going on. Years ago, before I got married and had my first child, I was signed to the Ford Modeling Agency in New York City. A stylist who used to work with SWV walked me into the agency because he saw model potential in me. I was five nine and a half and 129 pounds soaking wet, with high cheekbones and slender hips. I had some potential.

Prior to SWV, I did some local print work for some hair magazines and a few local runway shows. By no means was I the next Tyra Banks, but I did have fun modeling. I'd decided to take a little break from modeling when I couldn't land any jobs for more than a year. Fortunately, God had other plans for me. I went on to enjoy a great singing career as part of SWV. But as the saying goes, "Nothing lasts forever." SWV split, so I literally had to start from the beginning. Then one day I just felt like modeling again. I jumped headfirst back into the modeling world even though I knew I had a lot of work to do as far as my body was concerned since I had really, really enjoyed eating during the hiatus. I was tall, but hips run in my family. Generally, the women in my family are slim until they have their first child or hit twenty-five years old; I was twenty-six. I was a year overdue and expanding below more and more as the months went by.

Things had changed so much in the modeling industry since my first photo shoot. I was older and didn't have SWV to fall back on. The modeling world for me was like a bipolar friend who would call me one day and ignore me the next. The cruel modeling industry with its unrealistic idea of thinness often made me forget about my dreams of modeling. The large gap between rejections and landing a job made me forget why I'd wanted to model in the first place. In other words, at this point in my life, only surgery could make my hips model size. Everyone told me that I would be fine because I was a "celebrity." "No one will look at your hips!" people told me. Yeah, right. It's hard out there for "celebrities" as well as for everyone else. I will say that while being a celebrity can open some doors, only talent can take you through them. Prior to SWV, I had been rejected at most of the major agencies including the Ford Agency.

After about three months of long workouts and dieting, I was a lean, trim size six, and 136 pounds. I still had a few pounds to lose, but I was at least on my way. I had some new photos taken and went through the industry again. The second time must be sweeter, because after being rejected by the Ford Modeling Agency, at age twenty-six I was signed to the agency for two years. Give this one to the naturally hippy!

My return to the modeling world wasn't easy. I had to reacquaint myself with the language of the modeling industry, the walk, the posing, and the diet. Being onstage for so many years dancing the latest hip-hop moves kind of pulled me away from the proper posture of modeling. I was so used to leaning to the side and shifting my weight to one side, I think my body was conditioned to fall into my "lazy pose," as I liked to call it.

The biggest adjustment was my diet. I'm a junk-food junkie. I can eat junk food all day and night. Give me some

Starburst, Sour Patch Kids, Life Saver Fruit Chews, or anything fruity and sweet, and I'm in heaven. I love apple pie à la mode and I would probably donate a kidney for some soul food. Lord help me, if I could replace my husband with a plate of collard greens, turkey, and dressing, corn pudding soufflé, candied yams, baked macaroni and cheese, corn bread, and a homemade dessert, I would have no complaints. Honest!

I started doing a few test shoots to build up my portfolio. Test shoots are cool because there's no pressure. It's just you and the photographer, and you can be as loose as you want to be. No one is there to compete with you. It's wonderful to have someone tell you that you're beautiful and fabulous all day. It can go straight to your head. I felt amazing on my test shoots. But whenever I had to go on an audition or do a shoot with another model, I found myself player-hating . . . big-time!

I remember one particular test shoot that took place in a very large studio where there was another shoot scheduled for the same time on the other side of the room. There were two girls who were significantly younger and thinner than me doing the other photo shoot. I felt like hiding. They were absolutely beautiful. I started my session before them hoping to finish quickly so that I could sneak out before anyone noticed me. No such luck. Their photographer was running late, so lucky ol' me had the pleasure of having them watch my entire session. I wanted to close them out, but I knew I would want to peek in at them while they were shooting, so I let them stay. They made their little comments, such as "It would be better if you looked over your shoulder," or "Close your lips." My player hating was in full swing by the second pose.

In my mind, I was definitely the more seasoned model and they were too young to instruct me. But every suggestion they gave, my photographer loved. At that point, I was really ready to player-hate because they were stealing my adulation. I began to roll my eyes and pretend I was sleepy and hungry. I took a time-out for the bathroom only to sneak away to a phone to complain to my boyfriend about how I was being neglected at my shoot.

The girls finally began their own photo shoots, and they looked especially beautiful with their hair styled and makeup professionally done. I was even more pissed because I couldn't find anything wrong with them. I couldn't even make up anything. Damn it! So, I looked for another outlet; I started on the photographer. I felt he was very unprofessional and rude. He wasn't attentive to his clients and just a poor photographer, in general. Of course I didn't say that to him, but I was screaming every word of the thoughts in my head. I vowed to never shoot with him again. I couldn't wait until it was over so that I'd never have to see him again.

About two weeks later, I got the pictures back from that shoot. To my surprise and amazement, they were gorgeous. It was definitely some of my best work. I was a little ashamed of myself, because all of the comments of the younger girls had helped me make the best of my shoot. They showed me how to position my hips to make my body look more slender and elongated, which really helped a lot with my "family trait" taking up so much camera space. If they hadn't been there, I probably would've had just an okay photo shoot. Their suggestions and the photographer's cooperation helped me make the best of my shoot.

Shortly after that photo shoot, I ran into one of the young models in Manhattan. This time was totally different; I was extremely happy to see her. I'm sure she thought of me as a little moody, seeing how my attitude was clearly different from the last time we were together. We exchanged numbers and set a time to have lunch. She's now one of my good friends. I felt bad about my behavior during that test shoot, but it just felt sooo good to player-hate.

> "If there's one thing I can't stand it's some girl trying to tell me what to do. I feel like if I don't ask you for help, don't offer it. I start player-hating when I feel like someone is trying to boss me around. I'm a natural-born hater!"
>
> CAROLINE, *Florida*

I can relate, Caroline, but sometimes good advice comes from the last person you'd suspect. I almost lost some valuable advice because I didn't want to take it from some young girls who intimidated me. It might be helpful if you evaluated the advice first then decide whether it is needed.

I remember one time I had a "go see" for a designer runway fashion show. I had never really walked in a major runway fashion show before. I had been in a few fashion shows for clothing lines like FUBU and Tommy Hilfiger, but it was always as a celebrity model. In other words, no one was expecting much from me.

Well, whatever I thought I was doing before was noth-
ing compared to the way those girls were strutting their
stuff across the floor. They had attitude, confidence, and,
on top of that, more grace than you have at Sunday din-
ner. I, on the other hand, had to walk back and forth sev-
eral times before I even slightly got it right. Since I was
feeling so insecure, naturally, I had to player-hate. I had
to! It was the only way I could convince myself to stay
there and relearn how to strut my stuff. So I criticized the
designer. "She's just used to her favorites. She's only criti-
cizing me because I'm a celebrity model. Plus, her clothes
aren't all that great anyway." Even though I knew she just
wanted what was best for her fashion show, I was not
happy that I needed extra work on my step and so I turned
my anger on her and everyone else. Every girl who walked
in there that day was bait for my player hating: I couldn't
seem to stop myself!

First, there was this really tiny Caucasian girl. She had
blond hair and she couldn't have been any bigger than a
size two. I hated her! She came in, slipped on her dress,
and glided across the floor like she was actually doing the
show rather than just rehearsing. I was sick. The designer
had no complaints about her, but I sure did! "She isn't pretty
enough, she has no shape at all, nothing but bones; and her
hair needs a trim." As far as I was concerned, she was not
good enough to be in the show. Thinking this way made me
feel good temporarily. One by one, each more beautiful than
the last, these girls came in and they were all on point. Be-
fore the birth of my son, I was not a *big* girl, my weight

would fluctuate between 145 to 155 pounds, but next to them, I might as well have been obese! Bony wenches!

I was beginning to think about dropping out of the show when I caught myself. I was feeling like a fat, ugly pig. Then it dawned on me. I can't be too far off from these girls, I told myself. Of course not, I was there for the same reason they were. I may have been a celebrity model, but there were celebrities more established and much smaller who modeled. I was there because I, too, was special, in my own right! That thought kept me there and brought me back every day to practice my strut until I got it right. Now when I do runways, I work it, baby! Just like those little skinny tramps. (Just kidding!)

Here are just a few guiding principles to live by that can help you turn around any player-hating circumstances. First, women need to become more secure and comfortable within there own skin. It doesn't matter if you're short and you wish you were three inches taller. Girl, buy some three-inch heels. Nowadays, you can buy sneakers with a large heel! Coordinate that shoe with a hot outfit and you'll be bumping your head on the roof. Try not to use your insecurities as a defense mechanism.

Second, be open to criticism. Not every comment is meant to belittle you. For every comment that distracts you, add it to your *compliment box*. Constructive criticism can be helpful. Open yourself up for improvement.

If we, as women, can incorporate these two ideas in our daily lives, there would be no reason to always ask, "Why her and not me?"

· · ◆ · ·

"My best friend and I are the exact opposite from
each other. I'm short and thick and she's tall and
skinny. Sometimes I wish she was a little bigger
because for once I want a guy to look at me first.
I find myself player-hating on her, but that's my
girl and I would die before I would let any harm
come to her."

DALE, *Ohio*

KATRINA: It is hard to be considered the big girl of the
group. That stereotype can play with your emotions and
make you angry at times. I have a question: Why is it that
there is always one thick-bodied friend in every group?
And why am I that person among my friends?

Speaking of skinny friends, I have a very personal story
of player hating on Tamara. I Player hateHER big-time,
especially when it comes to her wardrobe! And 155
pounds?!?! Are you kidding me? Hell, that's my goal
weight. To me, the woman has everything! I can only
imagine wearing some of the things she boldly wears. To
give you a better idea of my physical makeup, I'll share a
few of the adjectives and terms that have been used to
describe me: thick, big-boned, juicy, big mama, a little
meat on her bones . . . you get the idea. Yes, I am athletic,
I had a volleyball scholarship. The bulk of my thickness
lies in my thighs. So, the Player hateHER in me would de-
scribe Tamara as a skinny tramp. There are some things

she wears that probably wouldn't even fit over my big toe. And because of that, I hate on her!

Even though we can wear some of the same outfits, for some reason when it looks merely cute on me, it looks gorgeous on her. And Tamara, my girl, always lets me know just how I look, good or bad. Her reason being, I can't go anywhere with her if I'm looking busted. Whatever the reason, the girl can dress her ass off with little or no effort; and I hate her for it. Maybe it's her years onstage and in front of the camera with SWV that has given her this "gift." I take every opportunity I can to let her know it. I am definitely not an undercover Player hateHER. I purposefully let Tamara know right out that she makes me sick!

At the same time Tamara player-hates on me because of my athleticism. She grew up with three older brothers. Her older brother Henry was a football jock, but Tamara knew nothing about sports until she started dating athletes. I can't understand it. She had never even watched a basketball game until January of 1994!

I was fresh out of college and still very toned when Tamara and I started hanging out. She might be tall and slim, but she was born with two left feet. It still baffles me how even today people constantly invite her to play in celebrity basketball games. She couldn't make a basket if she was airlifted ten feet over the rim. Just to make herself feel better she tells me, "You're good for your age but you're still big-boned and your jump shot is off." What a hateHER!

The friendship that Tamara and I have has not at all been altered by us player-hating on each other. As much as we "hate" on each other, we also love each other to death, which is what we are trying to get all women to do. Don't take any of it seriously, and more importantly, don't let it cause you to develop insecurities about yourself. Even though I player-hate, I still have more than enough confidence in myself to know that I, too, have it goin' on. Tamara takes every insult I throw at her as a compliment, and I do the same. In the end, we both usually end up laughing. So the next time someone tells you that you don't have it goin' on, you just tell 'em "thank you!"

Ladies, let us also not forget the Player hateHERs who *think* other women have everything. Shortly after graduating from college in Texas, I moved to Atlanta and began a career in freelance film and video production. I started out as a production assistant, working on music videos. In the beginning, doing music videos was great. I met a lot of different people in the entertainment industry, worked with different celebrities, and I was invited to a number of industry events. I put in long hours doing numerous odd jobs for everyone to prove my dedication. And as I eventually moved up to producing, things were going great. I had a job, not necessarily steady because doing freelance work sometimes really does mean "free," but nevertheless it was a job, I made decent money when I could, and I was getting my bills paid most of the time.

What I failed to realize (at first, anyway) was how those outside the entertainment industry looked at my job. They didn't see the struggle. Most saw it as this superglamorous job, but, honey, that was definitely not the case. The end result that you see on television is a veneer that hides what goes on underneath. What you don't see is all of the hard work, drama, attitudes, and headaches that go on behind the scenes. I'm talkin' about the blood, sweat, and tears that go into getting the perfect shot, editing it, and getting it MTV ready. But I noticed that people started treating me differently. Both people I knew and people I didn't know had formed their opinion. In their minds, I had everything. Little did they know a sister was straight struggling! I pride myself on keeping my personal life private, so therefore I try to exude only positive feelings whenever I'm around people, especially when I'm working. Having all of the attention was cute at first, but then it kind of made me uncomfortable because my "friends" were treating me differently. I was the same ol' Trina, but all they saw was me working and hanging out with celebrities, and for them, knowing me was just as good as knowing the celebrities themselves. Little did they know that for me, as a production assistant, all I was probably doing was getting celebrities their coffee. I remember one video that I worked on for a certain rapper . . . my job was to sit right next to the director and as soon as he yelled "cut" go on set and collect the ten thousand dollars in small bills that were scattered across the rapper's desk. Right before he yelled "action" I would strategically throw the money all over the desk again. I really didn't have any clout on set until I moved up to production coordinator and eventually producer.

Initially, my "friends" started expecting me to pay for everything when we went out for dinner or drinks. I was broke, too, and when I would try to explain that I was broke, after they quit laughing they'd say, "Trina, you so crazy!" At the time I was living in a small studio apartment with no furniture! And the more I insisted, the more, in their eyes, I became a snob. I would tell them how it wasn't all that, and they would tell me how lucky I was.

I have to admit that through my work in production I have met a lot of people in the entertainment industry. But to me, it's all business, networking, a process. It really became worse when I moved to New York and became Tamara's roommate, or as they saw it, Taj from SWV's roommate. By association, I was thought to be living it up among the rich and famous in New York City. And when I didn't respond to people the way they thought I, or a celebrity, should, they would say I thought I was all that.

People would give me demo tapes, ask me to manage their cousins who sing, ask me to tell Taj to sing a duet with their stepfather's first wife's cousin, and so on and so on. Finally, I decided to lay low for a while. That was a mistake because then I was being "stuck-up and conceited." I couldn't win. The hating had already begun.

"You're changing; you're just not the same person."

"Why won't you let me borrow any money? Ask Taj."

"Can you get SWV to sing at my birthday party next month?"

Finally, I just started telling them what they wanted to hear. I listened to a few tapes, and told them I'd get back to them. Turned down a few management propositions because "I had too many things on my plate" and said no to requests for Taj because she'd be booked that weekend . . . again. The player hating subsided a little, but at what cost? I guess it's true what they say . . . "Don't hate the player, hate the game."

Five

SOS—
Scared of Success

Will Smith once said, "If you're fixated on obstacles they become harder to climb, get out of your own way." This is so profound because it is the reason why Player hateHERs lose their focus. A Player hateHER will focus much more on someone else's success than on their own goals. To a person who is already insecure, this can lead to a whirlwind of player hating.

KATRINA: Have you ever sat down with one of your girlfriends and exchanged ideas about your plans and goals, only to find out later that she secretly hoped that all of your aspirations would NOT come true? Well, honey, beware! This hateHER has no obvious telltale signs of who she is, and the way she finally reveals herself to you is usually by accident and without her knowledge.

All of my life I have had the drive and determination to be successful. It was never just a dream, I made it my choice to be great and I was willing to put in all the hard work it took to make it a reality. Fear of success is what stops some women from achieving greatness. Their fear is greater than their confidence.

> "I would have to agree that my fear of getting out on my own held me back for years. I used to criticize people for doing their thing until I realized why. I was so afraid to try something other than what I already knew that it made me angry. It wasn't until I took a leap of faith and started my own business that I truly found happiness. Now I'm successful and I always want to kick myself for taking so long to just be me."
>
> CLENCY, *Pennsylvania*

It is so easy to do when you make the commitment to *YOU*! I made a commitment to myself to be the best me possible. I started in school by majoring in communications because I knew that I would need those skills to work in the sports and entertainment business. Then I surrounded myself with positive people like my family and my best friends, who encouraged me to reach for my dreams. Having the support that I did helped me to overcome many of the setbacks that I had to endure during my pursuit for success.

In my line of work, contacts and networking is vital. I

have had so much "funny" luck with some female contacts. For instance, there is a young lady whom I have known for a very long time. Let's call her Kelly. Kelly saw how determined I was to grow my business. She would even tell me she admired my persistence, but for some reason I could not stop feeling as if Kelly secretly did not want me to attain the success I had been working toward all these years. Every time I would pursue an opportunity to advance my career with my management company, it seemed as if Kelly would try to talk me out of it. A couple of times I even considered staying in my "secure" job as a high school teacher collecting a decent, but steady paycheck . . . because after talking to Kelly it seemed like the right thing to do. There's nothing wrong with maintaining a nine-to-five, but I was dead set on working for myself. It was all I had ever dreamed of.

One particular incident still bothers me to this day whenever I think about it. Marcus, a close friend of mine and an up-and-coming motivational speaker at the time, called and asked if I would consider managing him. I considered this to be a great opportunity, so I agreed to help him out with booking his speaking engagements. I enjoyed this work so much that I created my own management and consulting firm, specializing in the areas of sports and entertainment. And in 2002, I left Maryland and moved to Austin, Texas, to start my own business. PRO-TENTIAL Management was officially born and has since grown into a top-notch firm representing a diverse roster of clients including professional athletes, motivational speakers, corporations, and musicians.

I'd always felt that I could start my own business and everything I did before forming my own company was just preparation. Tamara and I discussed forming a partnership years ago. We wanted to create a record label that would promote great music for real artists, not the "Making the Band" artists that are flooding the airwaves now. We also had dreams of becoming fashion designers by creating a clothing line for the curvy woman.

We sat down many days and discussed big, big plans for the future and today we are living that future. We both have had several detours along the way, but we never ever gave up or thought that we weren't going to achieve our goals. However, we did recognize where our support did and did not come from and we picked up on the subtle hints of jealousy from some of our friends.

And I don't think it's so much that they didn't want us to succeed as it is they were projecting their own fears and insecurities upon us. For example, someone with low self-esteem and an insecure attitude does not possess the determination it takes to do some of the things I have set out to do and completed. What they don't know is that in spite of my fears, I tried. And that's the first step.

> "I don't have many friends, especially female friends. I find that females are usually jealous and judgmental. I think it is better to just be alone than deal with all of the nonsense."
>
> FLORA, *Florida*

Unfortunately, Flora can't recall a positive female relationship to draw strength from. After corresponding with her, we learned that she doesn't have a great relationship with her mother and doesn't have any sisters. This could be a big part of her unfortunate attitude toward women. It is possible that Flora doesn't feel comfortable interacting with women because she's never really had to.

When you have a bad experience—or should we say a player-hating experience—with a female not everyone will react the same or feel the same as you, so be mindful. Another thing to think about: when others hear good news, they may pat you on the back, give you a hug, and congratulate you over and over as if they, too, had achieved this success. But the Player hateHER appears to be reserved, smiles (fake), and says something such as: "That's nice, has anybody seen my purse?"

TAMARA: Unfortunately, insecurity is innate for many women. Some of us are more sure of ourselves than others, but we are all insecure in some way.

During my time in the entertainment industry, my upbeat personality always stood out. I was always considered the "nice one" in SWV. I didn't have the strongest voice, but my positive attitude helped me stay afloat in the music business. I could make the devil feel loved. This didn't always sit well with the other members of the group. They often felt like they were being criticized and that no one ever saw my indiscretions. And the other girls began to resent me. Sometimes it would get ugly. Let's just say I spent many nights alone in my bunk on our tour bus just to have a break from all of the venom that was being spit.

One girlfriend of mine, I'll call her Toni, told me about how she thought she'd found a good friend in someone only to find out that this so-called friend was out to get her from day one. Toni told me that this "friend" disguised herself very well. No one could tell her she was not on the straight and narrow. She called Toni daily, they would go out clubbing together, and it seemed like she was always there for her when Toni needed someone to confide in. Toni couldn't ask for more. So she thought!

Toni learned the hard way that every chance this "friend" could get to dog out Toni, she would take it. At the same time this "friend" would talk about her behind her back. This girl actually told people that Toni had herpes! That was a low blow. When Toni tried to discuss the situation with this person, she became rude and defensive. I told Toni the bottom line was that her friend was jealous of her for some insane reason and that she needed to get as far away from her as possible. Until this girl realized that she had personal issues, she would always project her insecurities and fears onto someone else. In this girl's mind, it was always someone else who was wrong and not her.

I understand where a lot of Toni's alleged friend's frustration came from, so my sensitive side would try to be there for her. This girl seemed to have plenty of friends, but she had been in several relationships that were not productive, her career was not working out the way she had thought it would, and she was heavily in debt. On the outside looking in, she resented Toni for following her dreams of opening her own nail salon. This is a classic example of "since I can't do it, I'll be damned if you do." This woman deliberately befriended my friend with ill intentions.

Player hating can be premeditated and obvious, as it was in Toni's story, or it can be covert. It is important to recognize the signs and deal with them appropriately. This leads to a very important point that needs to be clearly understood. Everyone makes their own choices. Some may be good and some may be bad, but ultimately one has to be prepared to stand behind every choice that one makes. Everything in life has its purpose. It's up to you to believe that the path you have chosen was meant for you. Most women love to play the victim when the choices they make do not work out the way that they expect. If another woman's choice seems to be more productive than your own, it can cause a resentment that can build into a messy catfight down the line. Learn to be content with the choices that you make whether good or bad because life is really what you make of it.

> "I know someone who has decided to quit her job to pursue other avenues. I felt like I was very supportive of her efforts because I know how hard and scary it must be to start a business, especially for a black woman. After time passed, this person found herself under a little bit of pressure to get her business up and running. She started to take everything so serious. She didn't want to joke around anymore. She was

> **always snappy and her attitude was the worst.
> She hated on everyone around her because she
> was having a hard time."**
>
> CATHERINE, *North Carolina*

For Catherine, it's probably best for her to try to convince her friend to discuss how she feels about her situation with the people who are closest to her. They can help her get through her rough period. If she shuts out the world, it is easy to make a mountain out of a molehill. And we all know how women can escalate a simple no into a major "Hell NO!"

Nothing in life is perfect and you will run into some women who are just not happy with themselves no matter what. Don't let one bad apple spoil the whole bunch. Do not prevent yourself from meeting a really good friend because you met one person that can't handle a little adversity. Always foster someone else's talents and dreams no matter how outlandish they may seem. You may not be rewarded instantaneously, but good actions are always noticed and will be reciprocated in time.

KATRINA: Ultimately, the hateHER is afraid that someone else will have the drive and tenacity to do something she herself can't do. I have made several leaps into what I thought would be a successful career only to fall short. One attempt that comes to mind is the mail-order catalog business that I started and ended after a brief six-month stint. After receiving orders from no one but my immediate family members, I gave up. But from each of those ventures came a lesson learned. One Christmas Tamara got me a book on 101 careers you can start at home. I had to laugh because I didn't realize my drive toward entrepreneurship was so apparent. She knew exactly what I was trying to accomplish in life, and she encouraged it . . . without me ever having to say a word. On the flip side, I've had other friends who had direct connections to someone who could possibly advance my career, but they never once offered to initiate some type of meeting or conversation between me and the contact. All I needed was an introduction; no one can sell me better than me. And the rest I would do on my own.

Have faith that you will succeed, lift yourself up, but most importantly, lean on the friends who do support you. They will help you to combat the hateHERs, and every time they give an encouraging word, it'll be right on time. But at the same time, your player-hating friend is obviously experiencing difficulties and dealing with some issues. So don't cut her off, be there for her because she wants what you already have. On your way up the ladder of success, don't forget to turn around and reach out a helping hand to other women on their way up. There's room for us all at the top.

Six

Can't Judge a Book by Its Cover

Stereotypes afflict everyone. Blondes are airheads. Black women have attitudes. Jews are cheap. Those people from a particular side of town are bad, and so on and so on. Depending on where we grew up or the ideas of those who raised us, we all hold stereotypes about people who are different from ourselves. It isn't until we step out into the world on our own and are free to make our own decisions that we realize that our preconceived notions about other people may have been dead wrong. Some of the people we were "warned" about may become our best friends; or we continue to judge people based on someone else's experiences and we end up missing out on what could become strong and wonderful relationships. Judging someone based on preconceived notions has to be one of the worst forms of player hating. . .

KATRINA: When I pledged Delta Sigma Theta Sorority, Incorporated, in the spring of 1992 at Angelo State University in Texas, I had no idea how strongly it would impact my life. At the time I went to ASU, African-Americans made up less than 2 percent of the total enrollment at the university. I was the only black girl on the volleyball team; the rest were either Caucasian or Hispanic. And although we all got along really well, they could never understand why I needed to have friendships with other young women who looked like me. I didn't really know any of the other black girls that well because they were always huddled in a group, looking but not speaking, and I was usually with the other girls on the team.

The first black girl I met was named Lisa Wilson. Lisa worked at the front desk in the freshman dormitory. I would speak to her when I passed by the front desk, but to this day, she swears I used to look at her and not speak. I think we'll always have two different versions of how we met. But somewhere down the road, we did manage to become friends and eventually sorors. Later, Lisa would be the one to tell me that a group of students was trying to get the first black sorority chartered on campus. I'll never forget "the meeting" I had to attend with all of the other girls who were interested. I walked in and saw all the black female students whom I had for the past two years only shared general pleasantries with. You know, throw up a hand and wave or say hello, but typically, it wasn't much more than that. As soon as I sat down among these women, I knew this was much more than just an "interest" meeting. Just the fact that we were all in the same room was huge.

Now, this chapter touches on subjects that, whether they admit it or not, are extremely sensitive to women. On the next couple of pages, we are going to share Player hateHer experiences as they relate to skin color (light skin vs. dark skin), interracial dating (jungle fever), and appearance (your hair vs. your weave). As you read on, your natural player-hating mechanism might kick in and have you saying things like "she's lying," "that's not true," or "she's just jealous." But remember, we said these are stories from personal experiences. We are just sharing what we've witnessed from situations in our lives. We are not bashing anyone. Now that we've basically written a disclaimer . . . let's continue.

As I sat in this room with about fifteen other black girls, I was a little nervous. I couldn't understand why they would want me to be a part of this important mission to bring this sorority to campus when I hadn't really spent a lot of time with any of them. Over the next several months, I would see these girls *a lot*. We would criticize one another or talk about one another, but that was all short-lived. Somewhere in the midst of all of the disagreements, we continued to grow in agreement on the reason we were all there. And then we began to form friendships. We actually started to trust and listen to one another. And nine of us went on to become the founding members of ASU's first historically black Greek-letter organization recognized on campus. As founders of the Rho Nu Chapter of Delta Sigma Theta, we had become sisters. We bonded in a way that only the nine of us will ever be able to understand. The biggest impact could be seen around campus. Collectively, we were a young group of black women making contributions to our local community *and* we were seen regularly around campus together. By the time we finished the pledging process, we had bonded and become sisters. But when I look back on it, I realize that it almost didn't come to be because a small group of girls thought, without really knowing me, that I was stuck-up and I behaved "white." They made assumptions without ever getting to know me. If it weren't for the few who, I'm told, fought for me, I might not ever have become a member of Delta Sigma Theta Sorority.

Fortunately, this example of player hating didn't affect me negatively. It's actually an example of how unity among sisters can be a great and strong force for good. Although we don't get a chance to get together the way we used to, I'll never forget the new family I gained when I crossed the sands on March 28, 1992, with my line sisters. Ooooooooooppp!! Delta Sigma Theta for Life!

Finally, there was an option on the long list of campus organizations for black female students who wanted to belong to a group deeply rooted in the history of African-American cultural life.

✦ Rita, from North Carolina, writes: The only reason I pledged Alpha Kappa Alpha Sorority (AKA) was because my mom and all of my aunts pledged AKA. I felt I had to pledge AKA or I would be disowned by my family, but all of my girlfriends at school were either Deltas or Zetas. ✦

✦ Nicole, a twenty-six-year-old teacher from Las Vegas, recalls how after constantly being singled out because of her light skin, she felt rejected by the Deltas and accepted by the AKAs. And although it wasn't apparent to others, Nicole writes, "I felt like all of my friends, both male and female, had made the decision for me. Even though I love my sorors and I'm glad I pledged AKA, the decision was made purely based on the stereotypes of others instead of on my own principles and beliefs. ✦

A couple of years ago, while sitting down at the kitchen table, I had a very interesting conversation with my grandmother, Big Mama, who at the time was about sixty-seven years old. My grandmother is a beautiful, fair-skinned woman who back in the day was considered someone who could "pass" for white, an attribute she did not enjoy at all, I might add. The reason Big Mama and I got on the subject of skin color was that I had asked her how her and my grandfather, Papa, got together.

Now let me tell you a little bit about Papa. He is a tall, handsome, dark-skinned brother and was very popular during his school days when he and Big Mama met. What

I found most interesting about this conversation, which Papa eventually joined, was how in spite of their true love for each other, skin color was an issue. Big Mama told me that she didn't have many friends because all of the other girls picked on her because her skin was so light, and it didn't help that she also had a gorgeous figure. She was even spat upon, and called a white girl. However, Big Mama did not lack any attention from the boys, which I am sure did not help with her lack of friends and the name-calling. But Big Mama was able to find some solace in being with Papa. No one messed with her, to her face anyway, while she was with Papa. It was as if being with him made her "colored" and thus accepted among her peers. She fell in love with him, but I think that a strong part of her just wanted to belong, and being with him did that for her. Before my grandmother told me this, being the dark-skinned sister that I am, I had felt that light-skinned sisters got all the breaks.

Once I digested all of this, I called Tamara and told her that Big Mama had Light Skin Disease or what I refer to as LSD. The reason she was infected with this social disease was that, by our standards, she was able to win one of the brothers because of her skin color. And Papa confirmed this for me when he jumped into the conversation and told me that "he was the man" when he was with my Big Mama back in the day. He told me of one instance when he took her to a dance at the local Veterans of Foreign Wars hall and all of his friends were talking about him and patting him on the back because he walked into the dance with

Big Mama and not some "nappy-headed black girl." Gasp! I couldn't believe what I had just heard. I am that nappy-headed black girl! Papa had LSD, too. I quickly hit redial to tell Tamara how Papa was also infected with the disease. We both laughed and talked about how the whole light-skinned vs. dark-skinned thing is so prevalent and goes way back to slavery; unfortunately, we've always been divided.

· · ◆ · ·

KATRINA: Now let's talk about the hair. This is an age-old topic with black women, especially the ability to call out a woman with a weave. I have to admit; I was not blessed with the gift to spot a weave. But Tamara definitely has the gift. She can spot a weave, and a good-quality weave at that, from a mile away. Sometimes I have honestly been shocked that someone was wearing a weave; it looked just that good. Of course, I can spot the bad and obvious ones, but who can't? Most of my life I have worn my own hair however I wanted, or have worn braids because I didn't want the dramatic change that wearing a weave came with—or so I thought. However, after tiring of braids and everybody and their mama braiding their hair, too, I decided to try a weave, and now I'm hooked!

◆ Regina, a hairdresser from Texas, shared this story with us about her clients: "I love doing what I do! I do more than hair; I listen. And I get women from all walks of life in my chair. And the stories these women share with me about their lives has helped me to grow as a person. And the biggest lesson I've learned is: never judge a book by its cover. I admit that I used to stereotype people. I had one client who used to come in every week and step out of her Jaguar wearing Gucci designs and beautiful diamonds. She always carried a different Louis Vuitton bag, and who knows where her beautiful shoes came from. I envied her a little because it always seemed like she had it together and was living a great life. Well, after about a year of doing her hair, we became friends and started to talk about a lot more personal issues when she was in my chair. And though it appeared from the outside that everything was wonderful, inside she was a broken woman. One day she confided in me about her married life and we both ended up in tears. We left the shop and went to a happy hour and we talked until the club closed and we've talked every day since. The two of us have so much in common and share so much, but I almost missed out by judging her by the car she drove and the clothes she wore." ✦

KATRINA: Interracial dating or "jungle fever," as it is so commonly called, remains a very touchy subject.

✦ Carmen, a Hispanic woman from New Jersey, writes that she has never had any girlfriends. All of her friends have always been guys and she has always preferred to date black men. "I feel like choosing to exclusively date black men has made my own race ignore me. I know they're just jealous, but I choose my own happiness over what others may think." ✦

In the past, when I have seen a white woman with a black man, one of two thoughts would immediately pop into my head: "What is he doing with her?!" Or "She can have him, he's ugly!" And this is player hating in all its glory, because never did I once see these two people as a loving couple, caring parents, or even great friends. Since I myself was not in a committed relationship, I could only focus on player hating on her/them because I still hadn't found my own knight in shining armor.

However, I've since matured. I was once in a relationship with a young man who was half Caucasian and I absolutely adored all of the beautiful white women in his family. As a matter of fact, long after our relationship ended, his mother, sisters, and I maintained a very close relationship.

"My husband and I have not said two words to the majority of our family, including our parents. He is black and I am white and both of our families said that we would not be welcomed into the family if we got married. We've been married seven years now and our family consists of the two of us and our two daughters. I think we're better off without those ignorant people in our lives, even if they are family. We have two beautiful little girls and it bothers me that they don't have grandparents, but I refuse to have them around my parents if they can't accept my husband."

ANONYMOUS

I learned so many lessons while dating him, but the one that has stuck with me the most is that skin color has absolutely no bearing on your capacity to love another human being. If a man makes a woman happy, no matter his color, then that's what's important. My opinion about interracial dating changed so quickly; just because you player-hate at one time or another does not mean that you are and forever will be a Player hateHer. If I can change, you can, too.

TAMARA: I have a different tale of relationship player hating. My husband and I have known each other since 1994, dated since 1998, and got married in 2004. Not to toot my own horn, but my husband, Eddie George, is fine! I'm fortunate to be able to say that I found one of the good ones. He's six three and 240 pounds of pure man. He had a great NFL career, has been honored with all kinds of accolades, is very intelligent, and is passionate about his family, not to mention extremely romantic. He's just a real stand-up kind of guy and I'm so blessed that he loves me.

I've been guilty of assuming a cute guy should be with a supercute girl, but I've never hated or disrespected a woman because of her man. My husband is also a private person. Few people ever truly knew what he was up to. So it caught most of his fans off guard to find out that he actually had a steady girlfriend. Then, when they found out it was me, I came under attack from many of his female fans. Not everyone was rude but a lot of them felt it was necessary to pick apart my appearance and everything else about me. I believe many of his female fans expected him to have a trophy on his arm. You know the type, the kind of woman that looks too good to be true. Don't get me wrong, I've had my pick of the litter myself. I've always had a boyfriend and never had a problem attracting a man. I've also never had to make the first move. Every boyfriend I've had has always pursued me. I often visited Eddie's Web site to conduct research for this book because the women provided me with so much useful information. On the Web site there was a message board that allowed his fans to post comments about anything that they wanted. Eventually the message board took on a life of its own. It became the place to find confirmed gossip about anything and everyone. There would be "eFights" and swirls of "eArguments" every day on those boards. I figured the best place to begin researching this chapter would be to go to a place where a bunch of women could anonymously speak freely about how they really felt. Thanks, ladies!

I was shocked at what these women thought of me. I had never met any of them and couldn't pick them out of a lineup if their mothers helped me. Yet they knew every move I made and criticized everything about me. As far as these women were concerned, I was ugly and would never be good enough for their Eddie. They couldn't understand what Eddie saw in me. They even assumed that it must have been a rumor that we were dating because he was too good to be with a person like me. WOW! Who were these people? Our engagement was unfathomable to them. Finally, they decided it was one of two things: I was pregnant and by marrying me he was merely doing the right thing, or because he was turning thirty and his career was coming to a close, he was panicking. I'll never forget the real kicker:

"Eddie only married Taj because he's really bisexual and the marriage is to help hide his secret . . . she doesn't even know!"

POSTING AT WWW.EDDIEGEORGE.COM

Never did these critics ever stop to think that maybe he was in love. I've come to realize that I'm in a no-win position when it comes to my husband—a successful, high-profile man. Any woman with a good man is in the same position. It doesn't matter what you do, how you look, or whose life you may have saved, as long as you're with someone who is doing more than warming up the sofa, you will be criticized and hated on.

Stay clear of criticizing others; it's only an outward manifestation of your insecurities. Only a woman who doesn't think that she is capable of doing anything out of the ordinary will hate on a woman who has attempted to achieve the extraordinary. Believe that you are beautiful and special. You are capable of having whatever and whoever you want. Please don't go after anyone else's man, but know that you can have the best of the best as long as they are available!

Seven

Relatively Speaking

TAMARA: *My mother used to tell me, if family members* are pitted against one another, they will hurt you worse than any enemy ever could. Your family may not intentionally hurt you, but they can be jealous, angry, conniving, and cruel just like anyone else. One of the biggest sources of family feuds will always be between a mother and her son's girlfriend and/or wife. Why is that? I've always said that if I ever have a son, I would not treat his girlfriends improperly. Typically, we think fathers are hard on their daughters' boyfriends, but many mothers have said those same words and have come up short when their baby boy has brought home a young lady who didn't meet their expectations. Isn't it funny that a guy's mom could love everything about a young lady until she starts dating her baby boy?

✦ Paul of New Jersey had known a young lady for about six years. His mom never had a complaint about her until the two of them began dating. There was an incident when he and his girlfriend were kissing on the porch. His mother came outside and told them that they were acting like children and that someone might see them kissing. They argued because he was a twenty-five-year-old man with a job. The atmosphere between his girlfriend and his mom became so strained that the two of them stopped speaking. In the end, the strain of having to choose between his family and his girlfriend became so stressful that the once happy couple broke up. He really cared for her but didn't want to date anyone his family couldn't get along with. Love eventually brought them back together, but the relationship was in limbo for several years. ✦

Ironically, I was in a similar situation for a few years. On June 20, 2004, I became Mrs. Edward N. George Jr. This was no small feat. Eddie is an only boy, and the women in his family can be very overprotective of their men. From day one I didn't stand a chance with them because they had already decided that no woman would ever be good enough for their Eddie. They never gave me a chance to prove to them I was a good woman.

You never want to create a situation where the guy has to choose between his girlfriend and his mother. Never once did I do that to Eddie. I knew how close he and his mother were and the last thing that I wanted was for them to fight over me. I was just his girlfriend at the time, and our relationship could have easily been terminated while his mother would be there forever. Keeping that in mind, even at our worst hour I never once disrespected his mother. In spite of her repeated attempts to ignore my presence, Eddie would always make an effort to include me in his family life and that only gave her more reason to dislike me. In public, she never introduced me to anyone, never talked directly to me; she treated me as if I were a peasant and always made it a point to let others know she believed that I was just a gold digger who would never have a future with her son. I believed that made Eddie fall deeper in love with me because whenever he would hear about how rude his mother was, he made it a point to let me know how much he really cared for me. In the long run it was easier for her and me to resolve our differences because the one thing we've always had in common is that we both want what's best for Eddie.

During our first year together, I went to his family reunion. While most of the older women in the family were putting away the food and cleaning up, Eddie walked me over to his grandmother and a few of his aunts and introduced me by saying: "Hey, Grandma, everybody! This is my girlfriend Tamara!" All I can remember is a loud voice

saying "Your *what*?" I was frozen. There was nary a hello
or any warmth. His grandmother, whom I had met a few
times before, decided she couldn't remember me. If you've
ever felt so uncomfortable it caused a lump to form in your
throat, you might have an idea of how I felt. I didn't know
what to say after that. Finally, his aunt formally intro-
duced herself to me. She told me that Eddie was their baby
and that just anybody couldn't be with him, and she even
took it upon herself to say that I must be a nice girl since
he'd brought me to the family reunion, and it was a plea-
sure to meet me. The family members closer to my age
were a little more welcoming, but it was the older women
whom I had to make a good clean impression on.

His mother and I went through years of strenuous ups
and downs. I had to remember that she didn't dislike me
per se; she disliked the idea that someone else had cap-
tured her only baby boy's heart. Now she'd have to share
the love. She was used to being the person he turned to for
everything. He had never really had a serious girlfriend.
As a matter of fact, I don't recall him ever having a girl-
friend for more than two years. I was lucky. I believe that
no one in his family was expecting him, at the height of
his NFL career, to find a serious girlfriend. Anything that
bothered my future mother-in-law about me was magni-
fied after we started dating seriously and she could see
that I was there for the long haul. She even told the pro-
ducers of the reality show that we were filming, *I Married
a Baller,* that when Eddie and I first started dating she
thought I was a gold digger! I could do nothing right. Nor
could she stand any of my friends. Not only was she nasty

to me, but she was usually just as mean to my girlfriends. If we were all in town for one of Eddie's games or just hanging out at the house, I would always introduce my friends to Eddie's mother, but that was just a waste of time because she always greeted them halfheartedly and then completely ignored them. Now that we are family, it does not behoove me to go into intimate detail about our transgressions; but believe me when I say it was not a very friendly environment. By the grace of God we have learned to overcome our differences and now, instead of fighting against each other, we fight together for our family. This has also made it so much easier for Eddie to enjoy both my company and his mother's together.

Based on our experiences, here's our advice when it comes to family feuds:

Step 1
EVALUATE THE SITUATION

Since women are emotional beings, we tend to overreact in a situation instead of evaluating it. Remember, there is always an explanation for everything. Even if the explanation is not what you might want to hear, there is always one to be found. Take a few minutes to cool down, then ask yourself: Do I really need to get upset about this incident? Can it be resolved without a major confrontation? Can I speak to this person without them becoming offended? And, most importantly, am I at fault? There are always two sides to every story, so be open to the fact that maybe you did do something to cause this situation.

If it's something that can be worked out peacefully, talk to the person and tell them how you feel. That person should be able to respect your maturity and reciprocate. A Player hateHER will assume that they are never wrong and that you are overreacting. If this is so, follow step 2.

Step 2
BE PROFESSIONAL, NEVER DISRESPECTFUL

It is so easy for two parties to argue and fight about truly nothing, but in reality no one really wins, and the losses can be huge. Aside from embarrassment, a public display of disrespect can cause you to lose your dignity and the respect of your peers. By choosing to always maintain a certain level of professionalism, you can actually prevent yourself from sinking down to the level of someone who is disrespecting you in front of others. In the long run, the negative consequences of acting out could far outweigh the temporary satisfaction you may feel by putting someone else down.

It is especially important to be respectful when the person one is feuding with is your boyfriend's mother. You always want to avoid creating a situation where the guy has to choose between his girlfriend and his mother.

Step 3
DON'T GET EMOTIONAL

When arguing with another woman, try to express yourself in a manner that is not offensive. Women can be very emotional and are easily offended. Use a tone that is warm and neutral. If two people are angry at the same time with no one mediating between them, things are bound to escalate. Statements can easily be misconstrued by the mere tone of someone's voice in uttering them. Compound that with body gestures and POW! Instant explosion! Be careful to use a tone that doesn't insinuate anger or frustration. A good way to break the ice is to take a person to lunch or invite them to your house. A home is usually the safest place to meet because it offers calm surroundings. Phone calls and e-mail can be impersonal.

Step 4
ALWAYS CONSIDER SOMEONE ELSE'S FEELINGS

It's so easy to think about how much someone has hurt *you* and why *you* deserve special attention. Make smart decisions. But try to consider someone else's feelings in a dispute. Wouldn't you rather be the person who steps up and shows some maturity and willingness to resolve a conflict than the one who's whining for attention?

• • ✦ • •

These steps are simple enough to resolve most conflicts. There is always room for improvement, but when two people care about each other as family and close friends should, nothing is insurmountable.

Eight

The Wedding-Bell Blues

KATRINA: *Throughout this book I have mentioned that I,* at times, have player-hated. Well, at the time of Tamara's wedding, I and a few of her other bridesmaids (Mona, LeLee, Nicole, and Gwen) were Player hateHERs not only during the days leading up to but even on the day she and Eddie got married. It all started the day before Tamara's bachelorette party. As Mona, Nicole, Gwen, and I were traveling all over New York City and New Jersey gathering things for the big day, the conversation would always come back to Tamara and how happy she was and how perfect her life appeared to be at that moment. Not only was she getting married, but she was marrying a fine man. So damn her!

We all shared stories about the men we had dealt with or were currently dealing with, and they all fell short in some area or another. Every now and then Tamara would call one of us on our cell phones and that would only get us started again. All of us were genuinely happy for her; there was no question about it. However, seeing Tamara in all of her happiness with her significant other made us reflect on our own lives and the lack of love in them. Every time Eddie looked at Tamara, we could see the love. Aaaaarrrgghhh!! We then moved on to the fact that not only did we not have a fiancé, but we were not even dating anyone seriously! So when would we (thirtysomethings) find our true love? Then I said it: "Tamara Antrice ain't shit." And then Mona chimed in with "And she ain't never been shit." "And she ain't never gone be shit," Nicole shouted. "SHIT," yelled Gwen. But . . . you gotta love her! We all laughed hysterically. I don't know if it was that funny or it only seemed that way because it was going on four o'clock in the morning and we were still making the chocolate penises for the party the next night. Throughout the rest of the weekend "Tamara Antrice ain't shit" became our mantra. One of us would shout it out while riding in the car or while getting dressed in our hotel room. We even shouted it out to strangers when we were at cash registers across the state paying for the last-minute extras. We went so far as to tell Tamara: "You ain't shit. You ain't never been shit. And you ain't never gone be shit. Shit. BUT we love you."

"Stop hating" was always her reply. Easier said than done.

Then came the wedding day, and I was the first to get my makeup done. And according to the compliments I received, I looked beautiful. Even though I still suffered from frequent spells of hateration, nothing could ruin my mood now that someone had called me beautiful. I was convinced I would get proposed to by a handsome stranger that night at the wedding, so all was good. That is until Lelee sat in the room proclaiming how great a couple Eddie and Taj were and that she wished it was she who was getting married. Well, so did half the women sitting in that room. Instantly, the mood changed to bittersweet. This situation forced us all to take a look at our own love lives. We were all doing well in our professional lives, but we all had a void when it came to love. Meanwhile, the heifer getting married that day didn't have a care. Lelee itemized all the things that Tamara had going for her that we lacked—the diamond engagement ring, the gorgeous gown, the perfect man, the European honeymoon! At that moment, we couldn't have resented her more! Then Tamara walked in and gave each of her bridesmaids a Tiffany bracelet with our initials inscribed on it.

"AAAAAAAAAAAhhhhhhhhhhhh" is all we could say. Needless to say, we were all embarrassed at how small and petty our feelings were, and how selfish. She was a beautiful bride and we all cried as we stood and watched her walk down the aisle. We cried for two reasons: 1) She was a beautiful bride, and 2) We were player-hating because we wished it was us.

"I have been a bridesmaid in five different weddings and I'm only thirty-four years old! Three of the weddings were my closest friends' and the other two were my sisters'. And I have one more close friend who is engaged right now. I hate to admit this, but when my friend told me she was engaged, I was not happy. In fact, I was jealous and even a little depressed. Of course I didn't let her know that. I did the overjoyed act just like I have the last five times I received news of an engagement. And when she asked me to be a bridesmaid, I told her I'd be honored. But at this point, being a bridesmaid only reminds me that I don't have a love life of my own. And I find myself hating on my closest friends simply because they're getting married and I'm not. I've been with my boyfriend for over three years, but I know he's not the man I'm going to marry. I think I just stay with him to say that I have a boyfriend. But of course I'll never admit this to anyone. I do my hating behind closed doors."

"NEVER A BRIDE," *Florida*

It is not uncommon for women in their thirties to feel like their biological clock is running out. The most important thing to remember is that you love your friend or family member enough to support them through their wedding even if its pulling at your heartstrings. That aspect alone makes you a great person who will one day meet someone who can appreciate your goodness. So relish your magnificent-ness!

• • ◆ • •

TAMARA: Ahhh, the joy of weddings! Weddings are a time when families and friends come together to celebrate the union of a man and a woman in glorious, passionate, and eternal love. That's the beautiful part of the wedding ritual. Then there's the not-so-beautiful extension of the whirlwind called your wedding day.

Are you familiar with the term *Bridezilla*? A Bridezilla is a bride-to-be who focuses so much on the event that she becomes difficult and obnoxious. Having been a bride, I can justify some of the stresses that come along with planning a wedding. For instance, when one of your bridesmaids tells you she's a size eight when she's clearly a size ten then promises to be a size eight by your wedding day. Of course, when the dresses arrive, she's half a size bigger than she was when she pledged to be a size eight, causing the bride to have to find a seamstress at the last minute. This can cause superfluous stresses on the bride that might force some less-than-princesslike behavior to rear its ugly head. Katrina can completely relate to that situation.

Your wedding day means more to you than life itself because this is the day that you become one with your soul mate. No one else will have more eyes on them than you, so it behooves you to make sure every detail is in order. To someone who is just a spectator, the bride might seem a little unreasonable, even bordering on unbearable.

"My bridesmaids called me a Bridezilla. I proba-
bly was. I didn't have a wedding planner to plan
my wedding. I did it myself. I don't recommend
this for any bride. It was so much to deal with
that it was hard for me to focus on the fun stuff
that comes along with getting married. I was
stressed all day every day until I got home from
my honeymoon. Maybe I was a little bitchy, but I
just wanted everything to be perfect and I don't
apologize for that."

JENNIFER, *Massachusetts*

I find it helpful to make sure that everyone involved
in the wedding-planning process knows what they are
responsible for during the big day. If someone is assigned
to the bride, be the best bride guard you can be. Even if
your only responsibility is folding the napkins, make
sure the napkins have the sharpest-possible edge. It
makes the day run smoothly if everyone is assigned a
task ahead of time.

Weddings usually bring the best and worst out of
people. They bring family members together who haven't
seen one another in years and friends who may have
changed a great deal during their time apart. That being
said, it is important for everyone invited or involved to
respect the changes that have taken place over the years
and those changes to come. Here is a small guide to avoid
creating a player hater or a Bridezilla:

1. **Everyone plays an important role**. Brides worry inces-
santly. If you are a bridesmaid, it is your responsibility to
make sure that the bride has no worries. Even if her request
seems absurd, bridesmaids should first cheerfully try to
calm her nerves, and then see if her problem can be solved.

2. **Prepare for everything.** The original definition of a brides-
maid is a woman who attends the bride at the wedding. If
you are a bridesmaid, try to foresee any potential prob-
lems in the preparations for the big day. If you know the
caterer is awful, or those red orchids might not arrive on
time, speak up! If you're able to prevent a disaster before
it happens, the bride will be eternally grateful (and might
even make sure you're the one who grabs the bouquet).

3. **Don't be a drag.** Even if you are starting to feel twinges
of bridesmaid jealousy, you must maintain your compo-
sure and relax. An understandably nervous bride will
make a terrible counselor during one of the most impor-
tant days of her life. So do your best to cheer up. Trust me,
she'll appreciate your selflessness.

When everyone upholds their responsibilities the
bride should be beautiful and relaxed. In the event that
the bride has many last-minute tasks to complete and is
being pulled in several different directions, it is very pos-
sible that a Bridezilla may emerge. When this happens it is
usually because a matron of honor or a bridesmaid has
dropped the ball. Now the player hating begins.

"When my girlfriend got married I wanted to choke her severely. She complained about everything. It seemed as if nothing was good enough for her. We all joked about how we were going to do an intervention when she came home from her honeymoon because we didn't want the woman who got married to come back ever again."

MARLYN, New York

A girlfriend can work her bridesmaids' nerves during her wedding. Hopefully you'll all look back at this day and have a good laugh. There are times when a wedding can cause so much friction that relationships are ruined. For whatever reason, be it a Bridezilla or hating bridesmaids, there may be some type of confrontation that doesn't have a happy ending.

"On my wedding day my bridesmaids were cool. It was my sister who 'hated' on me. She woke up with an attitude. I was trying to be nice, but after a couple hours of her bitching at my friends and everyone who came over to talk to me, I had had enough. She never told me why she was so upset, but it was clear that she was dealing with some jealousy issues. My sister couldn't have kids and she didn't have a boyfriend, so she was going to take it out on everybody at my wedding. I didn't curse her out or anything, I just pretended like she wasn't even there. Unfortu-

nately, we have not said two words to each other
since then."

CYNTHIA, *California*

It is regrettable that even sisters can succumb to wedding-day pressures. Learn to remove your personal emotions from the equation, kiss, make up, and move on. Life is too short!

Nine

Campus Envy

KATRINA: *I have been a student and worked as a teacher,* so I can tell you that player hating definitely occurs in a school setting. Whether you are in the teachers' lounge, the gymnasium, or the student center, beware . . . because the player hateHERs have also infiltrated the educational system.

The school-related player-hating saga that stands out in my mind occurred when I played volleyball at Angelo State University. I was offered a full athletic scholarship, which I graciously accepted on the basis of "everything being free." I had no trouble being spotted as I was the only black girl on the team. I truly enjoyed playing volleyball at Angelo State University, but there was definitely some player hating going on, both on and off the court. Off the court I understood that I was a freshman and that there was a certain rite of passage that I had to endure in order to gain the respect of the upper classmen. And I had no problem with that, but on the court it was an even playing field as far as I was concerned. I was blessed with the talent to run fast and jump high; that's why I received a scholarship. And I loved to use those talents, especially while playing volleyball. I'll never forget my first collegiate practice. I outshined everybody in the drills. I ran the fastest. I jumped the highest. I absorbed every word my coach said. And when we were taught something new, if I didn't understand, I would ask questions. My coach loved my enthusiasm, but apparently the other girls thought I was just a suck-up.

A girl named Diana was ahead of me in my position. Diana was a senior from Dallas and I had been recruited to replace her when she graduated. Diana was supposed to take me under her wing and teach me everything about the position and basically be a mentor. But immediately, I felt tension. In front of our coach, she showed me all of the drills and techniques, but when we were by ourselves she would barely say two words to me. I would try to engage her in conversation, but she was short and direct with her answers. Clearly she did not want to have any type of jovial exchange or camaraderie with me. At first, I thought Diana didn't like me because I was black. But that changed after I saw her and her friends in the cafeteria hanging out with several of the black football players.

Adjusting to college volleyball came easy to me. It wasn't too different from what my high school coach had us doing. It was just longer—we would practice twice a day for hours. I was getting better every day. I had found my rhythm and the coaches and the other girls on the team were constantly telling me what a great job I was doing. This only made me want to do better; I loved the praise. I worked extra hard because I wanted to play, and not sit on the bench. I had never sat on the bench before. Even in my first year of high school, I was moved up to varsity and started every game. So I made it my goal to become a starting freshman in college, too.

I had learned new ways to increase my speed and productivity and the results were obvious on the court. The swimming and aerobics I'd been doing helped my game tremendously. Coach was taking notice, and so was Diana. After a few weeks of practices, I realized that she had a problem with me. She began to speak to me less and less. Some days there was no exchange between us at all. Because we played the same position and we were in all the drills together, you could definitely tell there was something personal going on here. I was trying to take her starting position and she knew it! I had an obvious advantage over her from the first day that I stepped on the court: I could run faster and jump much higher than she could. She, however, was a senior and knew the drills, the plays, and the mechanics of the game a lot better than I did. But as Coach began to pull me to the side during practice to instruct to me on how I could improve on something, I listened and I improved. It showed, too. Soon the gap between my skill level and Diana's started to close. My teammates would pat me on the back and tell me how great I was doing—everyone except Diana.

As the season began, it got to the point where Diana and I weren't even speaking outside of our necessary exchanges on the court during practice. Diana felt threatened that her starting position was in jeopardy, and she was right. Coach had begun to put me in during some games, something that she didn't do with most freshmen. When I did go in the games, I replaced Diana, and she was not happy. Her parents attended every single game. I was amazed at how they would be at our hotel waiting for our bus in every city! And we didn't just play games in cities in Texas. We also went to Colorado, New Mexico, and Oklahoma . . . and they were always there. My mother had recently gotten a promotion at work, which took her all the way to Washington, D.C. So she wasn't able to come to many games, but she did visit whenever we had a number of consecutive home games.

Midway through the season, I had really learned a lot and my game had improved dramatically. My teammates even said that I should be starting in place of Diana. In practice, I would repeatedly outperform her. Diana did not like this at all. Even if we won the game she would be upset because I had been substituted for her in the game at least once. The other seniors played the entire game; she was the only one having to share her time.

I don't know if it was Diana or her parents who talked to Coach, but one day Coach called me into her office to talk to me. She told me that I had been doing a great job, had come a long way, and that I had a bright future. Then she went into this long speech about seniority and politics and what I call BS. She stopped looking me in the eye and basically told me that next year would be my turn and things would be different, but right now Diana was a senior and she had to play her, even though I was good enough to start. I was hurt, and she knew it! I couldn't believe what I was hearing. I wanted to break down and cry right there, but I was not going to let Coach see me cry. I told her I understood and then I hurried out of the office. And then I cried, not out of sadness, but out of anger. Things between Diana and me had gotten pretty bad. We didn't talk to each other and Diana didn't want any of her friends/teammates to talk to me either. I formed my own alliance with the other freshmen, who agreed that I should be in the starting lineup instead of her. I initially thought this battle between Diana and me would be decided on the court and that it would only be a matter of time before I was a starter. But Diana had taken things outside of the court and used her parents and her relationship with Coach to make sure she remained a starter.

Things were never the same after that for me. I thought it was unfair and I started to dislike the game. I was always told if you worked hard and never gave up, you could do anything. But this situation told me different. It showed me how politics and relationships can cause a situation to go in a completely different direction.

Diana seemed to have a little more pep in her step as we finished out the season. She knew what had happened. I played another year and a half, and as promised, I was a starter. But my love for the game and for the competition that I had gained all those years playing volleyball was suddenly gone. I didn't enjoy playing the game anymore. I started to resent the fact that I couldn't get to know my roommates and hang out at college functions the way they did. While my physical ability allowed me to still compete, I was just going through the motions. I didn't think she noticed, but my coach saw the change and told me that I didn't have that fire anymore. I lied and told her everything was fine, but the next day, after a lot of thought and counsel with my mom and brother, I went to her office and told her I didn't want to play anymore. She tried to talk me out of it, but she knew it had already been decided. Mentally, I had already stopped playing. Years later, my coach told me that the decision she had made regarding Diana and me was the worst coaching decision she had ever made and one that she has regretted ever since. I, on the other hand, continued my education without a scholarship and went on to receive my bachelor's degree and I never regretted my choice to stop playing volleyball.

TAMARA: I decided to go back to school to complete my bachelor's degree after an eleven-year break. Lord knows it was the scariest goal I had ever put in front of me. In the fall of 2002, I enrolled at Belmont University in Nashville and graduated two years later with a bachelor-of-arts degree in marketing. One of the biggest issues I had to cope with was the ten- to fourteen-year age difference between me and my classmates. Often I was actually closer in age to my professors than to my fellow students!

I never discussed my husband (at the time he was my

boyfriend) with anyone. I didn't look my age and that
made it easier to fit in, but other things set me apart from
my fellow undergrads. My husband has always been a fan
of nice cars. C'mon, he's a guy! I usually drove my Jeep
Grand Cherokee or my Mercedes G500 to school. Before
anyone knew anything, the assumptions about me were
out of this world. Some of the bolder girls came right out
and asked me: "What does your dad do?"; "How can you
afford two cars?"; or "Where do you work?" It was so
obvious what they really wanted to ask was "How in the
hell can you afford to drive two expensive cars and go to
school?" They didn't realize that I wasn't a child. I had
had a successful singing career that took me all over the
world. Sometimes I would be recognized as a member of
SWV by some of the African-American students, but this
was infrequent. In my opinion, the other students didn't
need to know about my background because I was there
to get an education, not explain my lifestyle to a bunch of
people I barely knew. I would answer their questions in a
polite but vague way and let them come to their own con-
clusions.

I was cool with allowing the other students to prejudge
me until I heard the rumor that I was dating a drug dealer
and living the fast life. I couldn't laugh hard enough that
day. I wanted to shout out loud in the middle of the cam-
pus that I've lived my life to the fullest and deserved the
things that I had. Grow up already! But the adult in me
just refrained from this. I figured that on graduation day
my boyfriend would be there and everyone would put all
the pieces together. A year before I graduated, Eddie de-

cided to surprise me by bringing me breakfast at school. It was easy for him to find me since my class schedule was posted on our refrigerator. He showed up at one of my marketing classes at eight in the morning with a big smile on his face and enough food to feed the whole class. Now my secret was out. Word traveled fast that Eddie George, one of the hottest running backs in the NFL, was dating the girl who worked over in the gym building. Isn't it amazing how some people change with the slightest information? Well, from that day forward I no longer was a drug dealer's girlfriend, or even Tamara. I officially became Eddie George's girlfriend who was in their class. I guess I have been called worse!

Ten

L'il hateHERs

KATRINA: *Children are born pure and innocent, with their* eyes honest and wide open to anything in their path. Caution is thrown to the wind in the mind of a child. Why shouldn't it be? Can you imagine the wrinkles on children's foreheads if they had to worry about all of the things that concern their parents? Botox would be a necessity at a very young age.

We received an e-mail at www.playerhateher.com from Jessica in New York, who told us that her daughter wanted to get breast implants for her eighteenth birthday and was determined to get them whether she and her husband approved of the decision or not.

Over time, the beautiful wide-eyed innocence of children dissolves into insecurity, their purity becoming tainted, allowing distrust to seep into their consciousness. Everyday occurrences in life shape the way we as people see the world around us. Children are not born hateHERs; they are created. My five-year-old goddaughter, Yasmin, absolutely loves baby dolls. But for some reason, she has it in her head that "brown" baby dolls are ugly and "white" baby dolls are pretty. She has received both brown and white baby dolls, but she still draws her own conclusion based on her five-year-old standards. In her five short years here on this earth, she has equated an African-American doll with being ugly and and a Caucasian doll with being pretty. This concept is already in her head and she learned it from someone outside of her own household. Her mother tries, now more than ever, to buy her African-American dolls, but Yasmin accepts them half-heartedly and clearly expresses a look of disappointment. As a mother, what do you do? Get her the brown baby doll because it makes *you* feel better or get her the white baby doll because it makes *her* happy?

TAMARA: It is almost impossible to protect a child from all that is wrong in the world, but a child's very first role models are their parents. The old saying that the apple doesn't fall far from the tree is true. Being a new mom, I have found so much joy in seeing how my son has inherited so many of my and my husband's habits (good and bad). I usually blame the bad ones on my husband's side of the family because there is no way that his undesirable behavior could come from me, but I'm sure my family would beg to differ on that much at least. The poor souls had to raise me and they know firsthand what a darling little girl I was *not* at times!

I know my son will have to deal with many issues in his life. But young girls have to deal with so many obstacles every day, then add on the many emotions and intimate female issues that come along with the whole being-a-girl thing, peer pressure, and we can't forget the biggie . . . BOYS!

> I am constantly having to go to my daughter's school because of all the catfights she is having with her female classmates, and she's only in the sixth grade! I keep telling her to be the bigger person and just ignore them, but these little girls are ruthless, and it's always about boys!
>
> ANGELA, *Virginia*

If a young girl is not prepared to deal with the challenges of negative peer pressure, boys, and all of the countless pressures society places on young girls, it's quite easy for her to lose her positive focus. That's where home life comes in. If parents allow their children to jump on the furniture in the house, those children will be prone to jumping on furniture somewhere else. Psychologists have proven tons of theories about parental influence on child behavior and written millions of books to back up their findings.

KATRINA: Girls are so unique. They are innately nurturing, sensitive, loving, and forgiving. These attributes are part of the driving force of this book. It is hard enough just trying to find your niche in life without having to deal with a menstrual cycle that disrupts your daily program once a month with mood swings, bloating, pimples, and cramps. And who can handle all of that when you have a classroom full of seemingly perfect-looking girls informing you that you have a pimple on your face? Anyone would run home and try every product in their medicine cabinet just to avoid being singled out.

TAMARA: The grass will always be greener on the other side for us as women and even more so for young girls. If we see someone who has light-colored eyes, we'll instinctively think that they are better than our dark eyes and wonder what we would look like if we had light-colored eyes. It's just a girl's nature to want to appear more attractive. It is also a woman-thing to always dwell on our own flaws; even the ones that no one else would ever notice.

Negative pressure is a big hurdle for young girls to overcome. Cliques form early in school, and girls tend to find companionship with others with whom they have a lot in common, but some will change their behavior to fit in with a certain group. It is within these groups that behavior is accepted or discouraged.

As wonderful as it may sound, Utopia would be a very boring place to live. If everyone was the same, behaved the same, and thought the same, the world would be dull. It is okay to have a disagreement. *Player hateHER* is our way of trying to promote a healthy way to disagree without malice. You should be able to disagree with your peers and not feel like you are being ostracized for your beliefs.

Katrina and I don't way want to criticize parents for their method of raising their children. This is just our report about what we have seen. Good behavior and the ability to make sound judgments start with good upbringing.

KATRINA: It is our suggestions that young girls today look to the positive role models in their lives to guide them through their journey toward becoming a woman and NOT the characters they see on television. Today more than ever, women on television are portrayed in an ugly way. We need to realize that the purpose of television is to entertain and not to teach. Let's challenge young girls by continuing to show them how the "sisterhood of women" is the best organization that they will ever be a part of and that player hating should only be a form of entertainment and not a way of life.

Be Nice

Be Nice. It's that simple. Yes, this book was intended to make you laugh, but more importantly we hope the player hateHER tales in this book help you grow as a person. If you can change something about yourself that is hurtful to others, challenge yourself to do so. If you're able to player-hate on another woman in a way that helps her change for the better and keeps your friendship intact, then do it. The authors of this book are proof positive that being a player hateHER and a best friend aren't mutually exclusive!

In addition, there are numerous organizations made up exclusively of women that are positive examples of how

we can get along and how we can be one another's greatest
inspiration and not one another's worst enemy. There are
sororities like Delta Sigma Theta, Alpha Kappa Alpha,
Sigma Gamma Rho, and Zeta Phi Beta. There are sports
organizations like the WNBA, Women's Tennis, and Women's Soccer. There are professional organizations such as
the National Chamber of Commerce for Women, Women's
Political Caucus, and even social organizations like the
Girl Scouts, and the YWCA, or you can always be creative
and start a sister group of your own.

No organization is perfect; however, those listed above
are a few women's organizations that are built on a foundation of unity, empowerment, leadership, and friendship.
And the Player hateHer Club was formed with those same
principles in mind. So, go to www.playerhateher.com and
join today!!

Celebrity Player hateHERs

Omarosa vs. Ereka Vetrini

Omarosa implied that Ereka was using racial slurs. After Trump fired her, Omarosa fanned the flames by claiming in interviews that Ereka used the N-word.

Uma Thurman vs. Daryl Hannah

Uma Thurman and Daryl Hannah reportedly asked to be kept apart when staying in a London hotel for the premiere of *Kill Bill Vol. 2* because they don't get along. According to a British newspaper, the two actresses mirror the animosity their two characters display in the Quentin Tarantino film, and made sure they were housed in separate wings of the Dorchester Hotel. According to the British newspaper the *Daily Star,* "When the arrangements were made for the *Kill Bill* party it was made clear that Uma and Daryl were not to be allocated rooms near each other because they often bristle and snap at each other."

Pink vs. Christina Aguilera

Pink slammed Christina onstage at her concert. While singing "Lady Marmalade" with blow-up dolls as stand-ins for the other three singers, Pink began to sing "you are beautiful no matter what I say" to the ugliest doll, and then started laughing. Pink had been planning on checking out Aguilera's after-show bash at a London nightclub, until she discovered that she wasn't invited to the event. However, she got her own sweet revenge on Aguilera when she told the bouncer at her album promotion party not to let Aguilera in the door.

Hilary Duff vs. Lindsay Lohan

This feud kicked off when Duff started dating Lohan's ex, Aaron Carter. Then Duff showed up at Lohan's *Freaky Friday* premiere, some say to intentionally upset her. Things really got heated when Duff realized Lohan was at the premiere party for *Cheaper by the Dozen*. Her mom went to Universal executives to have Lohan kicked out, but the execs said she was an invited guest and she could stay. This feud may go back even further as both were up for many of the same roles while at Disney.

Nicole Richie vs. Her Stepmom

Started up when stepmom Diane said she wanted her two children with Lionel Richie to be raised "normally, not like Nicole." Nicole responded by saying, "If you want a normal life, go get a job and stop asking for $300,000 a month," in reference to the amount Diane wants from Richie in their divorce proceedings.

Paris Hilton vs. Shannen Doherty

After Paris's sex tape was released online, Shannen Doherty was furious for Paris's dating her ex-husband Rick Solomon. Whenever they're out at the same clubs, these two always exchange words.

. . . and many more!!

Are You a
Player hateHER?

1. When you look at yourself in the mirror, do you
   a. See God's creation
   b. See all of your flaws but feel good about yourself
   c. Hate yourself and wish that you could change
      everything

2. You buy a designer outfit to go out on a Friday night. While out on the town, you see someone else with the same outfit. Do you
   a. Get pissed that someone else has on your outfit and
      talk about her to your friends
   b. Go home so that no one sees you
   c. Acknowledge the outfit but continue to enjoy yourself

3. You caught your boyfriend cheating on you. Do you
   a. Confront him and give him an ultimatum
   b. Blame the other woman and harass her
   c. Cut him and your losses by showing him the door

4. If you and your coworker are up for the same promotion and she gets the green light, do you
   a. Genuinely congratulate her
   b. Feel that she's okay but you would've been better
   c. Feel as if you deserve the position and stop speaking to her

5. Your favorite cousin falsely accuses you of being rude and conniving. Do you

    a. Try to talk it out

    b. Take a stance and argue your point to the end

    c. Curse her out and never speak to her again

6. Your mother-in-law is always rude to you. Do you

    a. Avoid her

    b. Ask your husband to talk to her and always show respect

    c. Be just as rude to her

7. You see a girl with great-looking hair. Do you

    a. Wonder if its all hers

    b. Ask her where she gets her hair done

    c. Find some fault because it can't be that good!

8. Your girlfriend announces she's engaged. Do you

    a. Genuinely congratulate her

    b. Feel like why her and not me?

    c. Offer your help planning her wedding but really don't mean it

9. Prior to your wedding, your husband's sister openly displays her dislike for you but has a sudden change of heart after the wedding. Do you

    a. Let bygones be bygones and welcome her sisterhood

    b. Tell her to go to hell

    c. Keep the peace while secretly keeping your distance

10. There's an overly friendly girl at your gym. She annoys you with her perkiness and you go out of your way to avoid her. One day as you're leaving the gym, the manager stops you and advises you that your membership renewal is past due. You ask to speak to a supervisor and it turns out to be Miss Perky herself. Do you

a. Pretend to be good friends and ask for leniency on your dues
b. Feel stupid that you didn't know how cool you could've been with the top dawg
c. Pay your dues and continue to avoid her

Scoring

1. a-0, B-1, c-2; **2.** a-2, B-1, c-0; **3.** a-0, B-1, c-2; **4.** a-2, B-1, c-0; **5.** a-0, B-1, c-2; **6.** a-2, B-0, c-1; **7.** a-1, B-0, c-2; **8.** a-0, B-2, c-1; **9.** a-0, B-2, c-1; **10.** a-2, B-1, c-0

15 Points Or More: CLASSIC PLAYER HATEHER!
You just can't help yourself. You have something to say about everything and everyone. In your eyes, everyone else is wrong but you. Fortunately, we have a group for you and a T-shirt. You are a player hateHER! Welcome to the sorority.

7 to 14 Points: WELL ROUNDED WITH PLAYER HATEHER TENDENCIES
You are a genuinely nice person who doesn't like to cause a fuss. You would prefer to keep your opinion to yourself most of the time. But at the right time on the wrong day, you can be clear about your feelings.

6 Points or Fewer: YOU'RE A SWEETHEART
You are a sweetie pie. You are the kind of person everyone else loves to hate. You will find the silver lining in everything. While others have something negative to say, you will always find the good in them. You're so sweet it makes everyone else sick! That's awesome!

ACKNOWLEDGMENTS

Tamara and Katrina would like to thank the following people for their support, in spite of the Player hateHers. First of all, we would like to thank God for being in our lives and in this project from the beginning; without His guidance none of this would have been possible. Ainsley Joseph of Imedia Idesign, thanks for capturing our vision with a fabulous logo. Darvis Griffin of The Web Park, thanks for www.playerhateher.com and your patience. Virginia Deberry and Donna Grant, thank you for the in-spiration. Trissa Watson and Debra Moton, thanks for fol-lowing up on our T-shirts. They are so pretty! We would also like to thank all of the people who DID NOT support us, or more importantly, hated on us because without you there would be no *Player hateHER*!

TAMARA WOULD LIKE TO THANK:

My family and friends for believing in me even when I didn't believe in myself.

KATRINA WOULD LIKE TO THANK:

First, I would like to thank my team: my mother, Cathy Willene Chambers . . . you are my best friend and my inspiration; I will love you forever. And my brother, Jimmy Lee Chambers Jr., your faith and support in me have helped me in ways that I'll never be able to truly express. You are my hero, big bro, and I love ya ta death! Tania, I'm so glad you're a part of our family, love ya! And to my nephews Trent "Rocka," Trey "Boogie," and Eriq "Woo"— Auntie Trina loves ya! To Jimmy L. Chambers Sr., I love you. To my extended family, I just want to say thank you and I love you. Especially Big Mama and Papa, Ma Willie and Papa. To all of my many aunts, uncles, and cousins in D.C., MD, and Kannapolis . . . I love you all. Uncle Keith and Fam', Uncle Mike & Fam', Teressa Dianne (TEAPOT), Aunt Betty, and Aunt Lottie, thanks for your constant support. To my short list of friends (you know who you are) . . . thanks for the support, especially Regina and Arnetta—I love y'all! Gwendolyn, Nicole, and LaMona— you were there for me when I needed you . . . thank you and I love ya! To my goddaughters, Taahirah Cherie and Yasmin Nicole, I love you soooo much. To all my sorors of Delta Sigma Theta Sorority, Inc., oooo-ooop, especially Rho Nu! Tamara Antrice Johnson George, thank you for being a true friend and helping me grow . . . my big sister, I love you . . . and Edward Nathan, thanks for giving me a chance . . . the sky's the limit! And last, but not least, I would like to thank and acknowledge God and His constant presence in this project, and more importantly, in my life.